WOME
OF TH
WORD

BIBLE
STUDY
SERIES

$\mathcal{F}$INDING
CONTENTMENT

SHARON A. STEELE

Gospel Light

Published by Gospel Light
Ventura, California, U.S.A.
www.gospellight.com
Printed in the U.S.A.

Aglow International is an interdenominational organization of
Christian women and men. Our mission is to lead the lost to Jesus Christ and provide
opportunity for believers to grow in their faith and minister to others.
Our publications are used to help women and men find a personal relationship with
Jesus Christ, to enhance growth in their Christian experience, and to help them
recognize their roles and relationships according to Scripture. For more
information about our organization, please write to Aglow International,
P.O. Box 1749, Edmonds, WA 98020-1749, U.S.A., or call (425) 775-7282.
For ordering or information about the Aglow studies and other
resources, visit the Aglow e-store at www.aglow.org.

Rights for publishing this book outside the U.S.A. or in non-English languages are
administered by Gospel Light Worldwide, an international not-for-profit ministry.
For additional information, please visit www.glww.org, email info@glww.org, or write
to Gospel Light Worldwide, 1957 Eastman Avenue, Ventura, CA 93003, U.S.A.

To order copies of this book and other Gospel Light products in bulk quantities,
please contact us at 1-800-446-7735.

ONTENTS

OREWORD

When the apostle Paul poured out his heart in letters to the young churches in Asia, he was responding to his apostolic call to shepherd those tender flocks. They needed encouragement in their new life in Jesus. They needed solid doctrine. They needed truth from someone who had an intimate relationship with God and with them.

Did Paul know as he was writing that these simple letters would form the bulk of the New Testament? We can be confident that the Holy Spirit did! How like God to use Paul's relationship with these churches to cement His plan and purpose in their lives, and, generations later, in ours.

We in Aglow can relate to Paul's desire to bond those young churches together in the faith. After 1967, when Aglow fellowships began bubbling up across the United States and in other countries, they needed encouragement. They needed to know the fullness of who they were in Christ. They needed relationship. Like Paul, our desire to reach out and nurture from far away birthed a series of Bible studies that have fed thousands since 1973 when our first study, *Genesis*, was published. Our studies share heart to heart, giving Christians new insights about themselves and their relationship with and in God.

In 1998, God's generous nature provided us a rewarding new relationship with Gospel Light. Together we published our Aglow classics as well as a selection of exciting new studies. Gospel Light began as a publishing ministry much in the same way Aglow began publishing Bible studies. Henrietta Mears formed Gospel Light in response to requests from churches across America for the Sunday School materials she had written. Gospel Light remains a strong ministry-minded witness for the gospel around the world.

Our heart's desire is that these studies will continue to kindle the minds of women and men, touch their hearts, and refresh their spirits with the light and life a loving Savior abundantly supplies.

This study, *Finding Contentment* by Sharon Steele, contains God's wisdom for maintaining a satisfied heart, whatever your circumstance. I know its contents will reward you richly.

Jane Hansen Hoyt
International President
Aglow International

$\mathcal{I}$NTRODUCTION

Jesus said, "I came that they might have life, and might have it abundantly" (John 10:10). Yet people today in all walks of life are dissatisfied, living in anguish with little or no peace of mind, no contentment. Even many Christians are strangers to the rich, full, satisfying life that Jesus said we could have. Although they desire a life of peace and contentment, they haven't yet found the way to achieve it.

Paul, the author of the Epistle to the Philippians, wrote, "I have learned to be content in whatever circumstances I am" (Philippians 4:11). As he wrote these words, the apostle was in prison for the cause of the gospel, facing an uncertain future. He realized his life could be snuffed out at any moment. At other times he'd been hungry, in need and in desperate circumstances, but he had learned to be content. What was the secret of his contentment in every situation?

As we study Philippians, we will see characteristics in Paul's life and principles in his teachings that led to this full, rich, contented life for him.

I would encourage you to put these principles into practice in your life and see what God will do. Malachi 3:10 encourages us to test God in our giving and see Him "open for you the windows of heaven and pour out for you a blessing until it overflows." I believe we can also test God with the principles we learn in this study. As we learn and apply them, we can expect God to pour out His blessing on us, meeting our every need. We will find contentment in Christ. We will experience the abundant life that Jesus came to give.

AN OVERVIEW OF THE STUDY

This Bible study is divided into four sections:

1. *A Closer Look at the Problem* defines the problem and the goal of the lesson.

2. *A Closer Look at God's Truth* gets you into God's Word. What does God have to say about the problem? How can you begin to apply God's Word as you work through each lesson?

3. *A Closer Look at My Own Heart* will help you clarify and further apply Bible truth in your own life. It will also give guidance as you work toward change.

4. *Action Steps I Can Take Today* is designed to help you concentrate on immediate steps of action.

What You Will Need

· *A Bible*—The main Bible used in this study is the *New International Version,* but you can use whatever Bible translation you are used to reading.

· *A Notebook*—During this study you will want to keep a journal to record what God shows you personally. You may also want to journal additional thoughts or feelings that come up as you go through the lessons. Some questions may require more space than is given in this study book.

· *Time to Meditate*—You will be working through a lot of Scripture in these lessons. Giving the Holy Spirit time to personalize His Words to your heart will help you experience the abundance of contentment and joy that can only come from Him.

How to Start and Lead a Small Group

One key to leading a small group is to ask yourself, *What would Jesus do and how would He do it?* Jesus began His earthly ministry with a small group called the disciples, and the fact of His presence made wherever He was a safe place to be. Think of a small group as a safe place. It is a place that reflects God's heart and His hands. The way in which Jesus lived and worked with His disciples is a basic small-group model that we are able to draw both direction and nurture from.

Paul exhorted us to "walk in love, as Christ also has loved us and given Himself for us" (Ephesians 5:2, *NKJV*). We, as His earthly reflections, are privileged to walk in His footsteps, to help bind up the brokenhearted as He did or simply to listen with a compassionate heart. Whether you use this book as a Bible study, or as a focus point for a support group, a church group or a home group, walking in love means that we "bear one another's burdens" (Galatians 6:2, *NKJV*). The loving atmosphere provided by a small group can nourish, sustain and lift us up as nothing else can.

Jesus walked in love and spoke from an honest heart. In His endless well of compassion He never misplaced truth. Rather, He surrounded it with mercy. Those who left His presence felt good about themselves because Jesus used truth to point them in the right direction for their lives. When He spoke about the sinful woman who washed Jesus' feet with her tears and wiped them with her hair, He did not deny her sin. He said, "Her sins, which are many, are forgiven, for she loved much" (Luke 7:47, *NKJV*). That's honesty without condemnation.

Jesus was a model of servant leadership (see Mark 10:43-44). One of the key skills a group leader possesses is the ability to be an encourager of the group's members to grow spiritually. Keeping in personal contact with each member of the group, especially if one is absent, tells each one that he or she is important to the group. Other skills an effective group leader demonstrates include being a good listener, guiding the discussion, as well as guiding the group to deal with any conflicts that arise within it.

Whether you're a veteran or brand new to small-group leadership, virtually every group you lead will be different in personality and dynamic. The constant is the presence of Jesus Christ, and when He is at the group's center, everything else will come together.

YOU'RE INVITED!

TO GROW . . .

To develop and reach maturity; thrive; to spring up;
come into existence from a source;

WITH A GROUP . . .

An assemblage of persons gathered or located together;
a number of individuals considered together because of similarities;

TO EXPLORE . . .

To investigate systematically; examine; search into or range over
for the purpose of discovery;

NEW TOPICS

Subject of discussion or conversation.

MEETING

Date _____ Time _____

Place _____

_____

Contact _____

Phone _____

ONE

TRUST IN JESUS

There is no other epistle that sings more joyfully than Paul's letter to the Philippians. His letter shouts with joy triumphant: "Come. Share my joy as you have shared my conflict," he invites. The fact that he knows that Jesus Christ loved him and gave Himself for him is the high note of his letter. Yet Paul wrote this letter near the end of his life when he was in prison.

What was Paul's secret? How was he able to trust Jesus when everything seemed to be going against him? How had he found contentment in such a negative situation? In this chapter, we will turn in God's direction. As we do, we will see Paul's complete trust in Jesus. It is only as we experience this kind of trust that we will find a satisfied heart—true contentment.

A Closer Look at the Problem

Even though we may not be in prison, we all face difficult situations. We live in a sinful world, and life is often hard. Not only that, but other people also seem to have it a whole lot easier than we do. How can we trust that God is really for us? How can we find true contentment and joy?

A Closer Look at God's Truth

The book of Philippians was a letter to the believers at Philippi, written by Paul from his prison cell, most likely in Rome. Paul had been instrumental in founding the Philippian church during his second missionary journey. The beginning of this church is the exciting story of how God can lead and use a willing servant.

Read Acts 16:6-10. Why didn't Paul and his companions preach in Asia or Bithynia?

_____

_____

_____

_____

What happened to Paul at Troas (see verse 9)?

_____

_____

_____

What did Paul decide to do (see verse 10)? Why?

_____

_____

_____

Paul had an intimate relationship with God. He not only heard what the Holy Spirit said, but upon receiving direction, he also acted immediately and in complete faith. What are some of the ways the Holy Spirit directs people today?

_____

_____

_____

_____

Read Acts 16:11-15. At what city in Macedonia did the disciples stop (see verse 12)?

_____

_____

_____

_____

Where did the disciples go on the Sabbath day (see verse 13)? Why did they go there?

_____

_____

_____

_____

Whom did the disciples find there (see verses 13-14)?

_____

_____

_____

What was Lydia's response to the message she heard (see verse 14)?

_____

_____

_____

_____

What happened as a result of her response (see verse 15)?

_____

_____

_____

_____

What a marvelous example of the work of the Holy Spirit! The Holy Spirit led Paul and his company to Philippi, and as they shared, the Lord opened the hearts of the women who listened. When Christians respond to the leadership of the Holy Spirit in sharing the message of Jesus, God will open the hearts of those who listen. Read Acts 16:16-24. Where were Paul and his companions going?

_____

_____

_____

_____

Who met them on the way (see verse 16)?

_____

_____

_____

What did she say about Paul and his companions (see verse 17)?

_____

_____

_____

How long did she continue saying this (see verse 18)?

_____

_____

_____

_____

What did Paul do as a result (see verse 17)?

_____

_____

_____

_____

Why do you think Paul cast this demon out?

_____

_____

_____

_____

By what power did Paul cast it out (see verse 18)?

_____

_____

_____

_____

Why did the slave girl's owners become so angry (see verse 19)?

_____

_____

_____

_____

What happened to Paul and Silas as a result (see verses 19-24)?

_____

_____

_____

Even though Paul and Silas were called to preach in Philippi, Satan attacked them there. Satan will frequently attack Christians who are obeying God's call. Sometimes, he attacks with little annoyances; other times, he attacks with huge problems or temptations. What are some ways Satan attacks Christians today?

_____

_____

_____

_____

Paul had power over Satan because he had the power of Jesus Christ available to him. Read 1 John 4:4. What is promised in this verse?

_____

_____

_____

What key to overcoming Satan is found in James 4:7?

_____

_____

_____

We too have the power of Jesus available to us. When we fight Satan in Jesus' name and in His power, we can win. When we resist Satan, he will flee. Share an experience in which you won a victory over an attack by Satan.

_____

_____

_____

Read Acts 16:25-34. What were Paul and Silas doing around midnight (see verse 25)?

_____

_____

_____

Who was listening to them (see verse 25)?

_____

_____

_____

Why do you think Paul and Silas were able to pray and sing after being beaten and thrown into prison?

_____

_____

_____

Paul and Silas were able to praise the Lord during this difficult time because they totally trusted Jesus. They knew He loved them and would take care of them, even though everything looked bleak and they were in pain

and discomfort. Their trust in Jesus gave them an attitude of praise and rejoicing. What miracle of God took place (see verse 26)?

_____

_____

_____

_____

How do we know that this was a miracle of God and not an ordinary earth-
quake (see verse 26)?

_____

_____

_____

_____

Why did the jailer decide to kill himself (see verse 27)?

_____

_____

_____

_____

What question did the jailer ask after he saw that all the prisoners were
safe (see verse 30)?

_____

_____

_____

_____

What do you think led him to ask that question?

_____

_____

_____

_____

How did Paul and Silas answer his question (see verse 31)?

_____

_____

_____

_____

What evidence do we have that the Philippian jailer became a believer (see verse 33)?

_____

_____

_____

According to verse 34, what emotion did the jailer experience as a result of believing?

_____

_____

_____

_____

The most essential ingredient in finding joy or contentment is that we, like the Philippian jailer, believe in the Lord. Until a person accepts Jesus Christ as Savior and Lord, he or she can never experience God's true peace and joy. When the jailer trusted Jesus to save him, he experienced the joy and contentment that only God can give.

Read Psalms 4:5-8; 16:7-11; 91:14-16; 107:6-9; 144:15. How does our relationship with God affect our experiencing joy and satisfaction in life?

_____

_____

_____

_____

When God created humankind, He created them for fellowship with Himself. Although we don't always recognize it, we are created with a natural desire, a longing, for God. Until we experience that personal relationship with Him, we cannot know the fullness of joy and peace.

The story of the rich young ruler who questioned Jesus about how to gain eternal life illustrates this point (see Luke 18:18-23). Although this young man was already living a moral life and had riches, he came to Jesus because he had a need—the hunger in his heart was unsatisfied.

Upon seeing the young ruler, Jesus recognized that this man's riches were the most important thing in his life. They had become his god. When the man decided not to share his wealth with others and not to follow Jesus, he went away in sorrow.

It's important to realize that the ruler became very sad because he had made the wrong choice. Jesus came to give an abundant life, but He cannot give that abundance and peace unless a person is willing to make Him the Lord of his or her life. Anything that we value more than God becomes, in effect, another god in our life.

What are some of the gods prevalent in our society today?

_____

_____

_____

_____

What are some of the gods in your life?

_____

_____

_____

_____

A Closer Look at My Own Heart

Paul told the Philippian jailer to believe on the Lord Jesus—in other words, to trust in Jesus. The young ruler trusted in his good life and his riches, and they were not enough to make him right with God. Romans 6:23 says that "the wages of sin is death." If we were to sin only one time in our entire life, that would be enough to separate us from God. Because the young man was not sinless, he could not find peace with God.

No one can be made right with God by worshiping or regarding as more important anything other than God, but God has provided a remedy for our sins. He sent Jesus, who was without sin, to die on the cross and pay the penalty for our sins. He takes our sinfulness upon Himself and gives us His righteousness (see 2 Corinthians 5:21). Our part is to trust Jesus to forgive our sins and receive Him by personal invitation.

Read John 14:6. What is the *only* way you can come to God?

_____

_____

_____

_____

In Revelation 3:20, what does Jesus promise?

_____

_____

_____

_____

According to John 1:12, what do you become when you receive Jesus?

_____

_____

_____

_____

Read Romans 10:9. What is promised in this verse, and what do you need to do to receive it?

_____

_____

_____

_____

Action Steps I Can Take Today

If you do not know Jesus as your Savior, you can know Him today. Remember His invitation in Revelation 3:20: If anyone will open the door, Jesus will come in. If you would like to open the door of your heart to Jesus, pray this prayer:

> *Dear God, I know that I can never have peace with You through my efforts. I am a sinner, and I am truly sorry. I believe Jesus died for me, and I trust that His death paid the penalty for my sins. I open the door of my heart to receive Jesus as my personal Savior and Lord. Thank You, Jesus, for coming into my life, forgiving my sins and saving me.*

If you sincerely prayed this prayer, where is Jesus right now (see Revelation 3:20)?

_____

_____

_____

_____

What did you become when you received Christ (see John 1:12-13)?

_____

_____

_____

_____

_____

What does God promise you when you believe in Jesus (see 1 John 5:12-13)?

_____

_____

_____

_____

If you know Jesus as your Savior, how deep is your trust? Think about the story of what happened to Paul and Silas in Philippi, including what is told in Acts 16:35-40. How does the trust they showed in God compare with yours?

_____

_____

_____

_____

Paul and Silas were in jail just long enough for God to do His good work in the lives of the Philippian jailer and his family. When they were thrown into prison, Paul and Silas did not complain and blame God. Instead, they sang and praised Him.

They were able to sing and praise because they knew that God was in control of every area of their life. He was at work and they trusted Him to do what was best for them. Because they trusted, they could rejoice.

Is there a situation in your life in which you need to trust God, especially because the situation appears hopeless? Write about it in your journal. Then thank God for the situation by praising Him for being in control of your life and working in your particular situation, even when you may not be able to see God at work.

Paul's words in Ephesians 3:20-21 will increase your faith. Write the verses on a small index card, and place it where you can see it each day. Each day relate the verse to your difficult situation, and ask God to help you trust Him more.

$\mathcal{P}$RAISE GOD AND REJOICE

A pastor tells this story of a couple who talked with him shortly after the unexpected death of their son.

> Early in our ministry a family moved to our town on a Monday. On Wednesday at four o'clock, their four-year-old son climbed up on the davenport and fell asleep. Not too unusual—but when they called him for supper at five o'clock, he didn't respond. The child had died.
>
> They called the doctor and the doctor called me. I met the parents for the first time. Tearful? Yes. Brokenhearted? Of course. But as they talked, something happened. They shared about what this son had meant to them and how much joy he had brought into their home. They told stories from his life. Thankful for the years they had had together, they asked God to help them through this difficult time.
>
> As I shared this couple's pain, I couldn't help but think, *My own son is the same age as the boy who died. If it had been my son who was taken, would I have had the attitude of trust and thanksgiving that they expressed?*

In this chapter we will learn how Paul's similar trust in Jesus gave him a grateful spirit toward God and others. Because of this trust, he was able to praise God and rejoice in the midst of trouble. We will also see that praising and rejoicing are important steps leading to contentment.

A Closer Look at the Problem

God commands that we praise Him and that we thank Him at all times (see Psalm 34:1; 1 Thessalonians 5:18). When we respond in obedience, even though circumstances look hopeless, God can use those difficult circumstances to bring glory to Himself and maturity to us. God did just that for the young couple who lost their son, and now whenever this story is told, men and women marvel at the power of God working peace and joy in the face of one of life's greatest losses.

When we praise God, we show that we trust Him, even if we don't see His hand at work at the time. Verbalizing our praise for a difficult situation releases the fear and anger inside us and allows God to bring something good out of it (see Romans 8:28). Yet so often, instead of rejoicing and praising God, we grumble and complain.

Read Psalm 106:13-15,24-27. What happened to the Israelites when they grumbled instead of rejoiced?

_____

_____

_____

_____

God was taking care of the Israelites, but they complained and grumbled. He finally gave them what they asked for, but they suffered physically and they spiritually moved away from God. When we complain about what God allows in our lives, we will be similarly affected physically and we will begin to wither spiritually. By contrast, when we rejoice, we will begin to grow stronger in the Spirit, and we will free God to take our difficult situation and turn it into something meaningful and glorifying to Him.

It is this same power of God working peace and joy in difficult circumstances that was experienced by the young couple whose small son had died. God did the same thing for Paul when he was in prison. He can do the same for you in whatever situation you might be facing.

A Closer Look at God's Truth

Read Philippians 1:1. How did Paul describe himself and Timothy?

_____

_____

_____

_____

The Greek word that is translated "bond-servant" can also be translated as "slave." What picture comes to your mind as you think of a bond-servant or a slave? To whom does a slave belong? What does a slave do?

_____

_____

_____

Read 1 Peter 1:18-19. According to Peter, with *what* were believers, including Paul, bought?

_____

_____

_____

It's important to recognize that because Paul trusted in Jesus, he willingly gave himself to God. When Jesus died on the cross, He paid the price for Paul's salvation, but Paul also made a choice. He could have chosen to remain a slave to sin with death as the end result. Or he could have chosen, as he did, to belong to Christ, receiving eternal and abundant life and willingly becoming Christ's slave. Read Philippians 1:3-8. How often did Paul thank God for the Philippians (see verses 3-4)?

_____

_____

_____

What was Paul's prayer filled with?

_____

_____

_____

Read 2 Corinthians 8:1-5. In this passage, Paul told the Corinthian church about the Macedonian churches. Remember that Philippi was the chief city in Macedonia, and you can see from Paul's comments to the Corinthians why he felt such deep love and gratitude toward the Philippians. What were the physical circumstances of the Macedonian churches (see verse 2)?

_____

_____

_____

_____

What had they done in spite of the trouble they were facing (see verse 3)?

_____

_____

_____

How did they look upon this act of giving (see verse 4)?

_____

_____

_____

What did they experience in the midst of their affliction and deep poverty (see verse 2)?

_____

_____

_____

How much had they given (see verse 3)?

_____

_____

_____

What had they given first (see verse 5)?

_____

_____

_____

_____

How did this sacrificial giving relate to their abundance of joy?

_____

_____

_____

_____

How did their giving reflect their trust in Jesus?

_____

_____

_____

_____

Read Romans 15:26-27. What was the Philippians' attitude in giving as described in these verses?

_____

_____

_____

Why did they feel indebted to the Jewish Christians?

_____

_____

_____

_____

A great persecution toward Christians had arisen in Jerusalem during this period. That, along with a famine, made life very difficult for the Jerusalem believers. The Philippian Christians were so grateful to the Jews for sharing the gospel of Christ that they wanted to share their material possessions with them. Their deep gratitude and their joy in the Lord resulted in a generous offering beyond their ability to give. In addition to aiding Jerusalem Christians, they gave generously toward supporting Paul in his ministry (see 2 Corinthians 11:9). One of the main purposes in Paul's writing the letter to the Philippians was to express his deep gratitude. How do you feel toward the person or persons who shared the gospel with you?

_____

_____

_____

_____

Do you feel that you owe anything to that person or those people?

_____

_____

_____

_____

Read Philippians 4:10-19. What was Paul's reason for rejoicing (see verse 10)?

_____

_____

_____

_____

Why hadn't the Philippians sent help sooner (see verse 10)?

_____
_____
_____
_____

What had Paul learned (see verses 11-13)?

_____
_____
_____
_____
_____

How much do you think Paul would have learned had he complained and grumbled instead of choosing to rejoice?

_____
_____
_____
_____

What effect do you think grumbling and complaining would have had on his attitude and his ministry?

_____
_____
_____
_____

How did Paul feel about the help the Philippians had just sent (see verse 18)?

_____
_____
_____
_____

What did Paul say would be the result of their giving (see verse 17)?

_____
_____
_____
_____

How did Paul think that God would view this offering (see verse 18)?

_____

_____

_____

_____

What was Paul's promise to the Philippians (see verse 19)?

_____

_____

_____

_____

In what way do you feel that the promise in verse 19 is related to the fact that the Philippians had first given themselves to the Lord?

_____

_____

_____

_____

In what way is the promise related to their generosity in sharing beyond their ability to give (see also Matthew 6:33)?

_____

_____

_____

_____

Read Philippians 2:14-16. What command did Paul give to the Philippians (see verse 14)?

_____

_____

_____

_____

What reasons did Paul give for the command (see verses 15-16)?

_____

_____

_____

_____

What effect does grumbling or disputing have on our witness?

_____

_____

_____

_____

What effect does rejoicing have on our witness?

_____

_____

_____

Complaining, grumbling and bickering can be compared to covering a headlight with mud. The light is still there, but it is so covered with mud that it is useless. A grumbling, complaining Christian will turn people away from Jesus. In contrast, a rejoicing, cheerful Christian will draw people to Christ like a powerful magnet. What does Proverbs 16:24 say about pleasant words?

_____

_____

_____

_____

What does Proverbs 18:21 teach about the power of the tongue?

_____

_____

_____

_____

Read Philippians 2:17-18. What circumstances did Paul refer to that could have made rejoicing difficult?

_____

_____

_____

_____

What did Paul determine to do anyway?

_____

_____

_____

What did Paul urge the Philippians to do?

_____

_____

_____

_____

Paul knew his life could be taken at any time. Even so, he determined to rejoice, and he urged the Philippians to rejoice with him. At this point in his
life, circumstances were difficult, but because Paul trusted Jesus, he chose to
rejoice. Sometimes when we really feel like complaining, we *must choose* to
rejoice. When we determine to rejoice and praise God, even in difficult circumstances, God will change feelings of frustration into feelings of victory.
Read Philippians 1:12-20. What benefits of his imprisonment did Paul give?

_____

_____

_____

_____

What two motives did Paul give for people preaching Christ (see verses
14-17)?

_____

_____

_____

_____

How did Paul feel about the fact that some people were preaching from
wrong motives (see verse 18)?

_____

_____

_____

_____

Why do you think Paul was able to have the attitude he had about those
who were preaching from impure motives?

_____

_____

_____

_____

What other reasons did Paul give for rejoicing (see verses 18-20)?

_____

_____

_____

_____

What confidence did Paul have in the Philippians (see verse 19)?

_____

_____

_____

_____

What part do you think Paul's confidence in God and in the Philippians' prayers had in his being able to rejoice?

_____

_____

_____

_____

What role do the prayers of others play in the life of a person going through trials? Share a personal example of this from your own life.

_____

_____

_____

_____

What was Paul's chief desire in life (see verse 20)?

_____

_____

_____

_____

What is your chief desire in life?

_____

_____

_____

_____

Had Paul's desires been wrong, he could have easily fallen into despair. However, he trusted Jesus, and his aim in life was to always honor and exalt Christ. Because exalting Jesus was his aim, he could rejoice and praise God right where he was. He knew that God was working in his life and that Jesus was being exalted. Again we see that Paul chose to rejoice: "I rejoice. Yes, and I will rejoice" (Philippians 1:18).

Read Philippians 3:1 and 4:4. What did Paul encourage the Philippians to do in these two verses?

_____

_____

_____

_____

How often did Paul want the Philippians to rejoice?

_____

_____

_____

A Closer Look at My Own Heart

Are there areas in your life that you need to praise God for, even though the areas hurt? List those areas right now. Prayerfully lay them before the Lord and determine to praise God for the way He is working, even if you cannot see His work. (You might even want to write "Praise" at the top of your list as a visual reminder to praise and rejoice.)

_____

_____

_____

_____

The psalms are filled with praise and thanksgiving. Read Psalm 33:1-3. What did the psalmist say about praising and rejoicing?

_____

_____

_____

_____

Read Psalm 50:23. What does this verse teach about thanksgiving?

_____

_____

_____

_____

Read Psalms 66:1,8; 81:1. What is commanded in these verses?

_____

_____

_____

What is the main theme of these verses from Psalms?

_____

_____

_____

_____

Psalm 33:3 speaks of singing a new song to the Lord—a new song that only you can sing. You can create your own song by writing a psalm of praise and thanksgiving to God. Look over the list you made of the areas in your life for which you need to praise God—you'll want to include some of these things in your song. Then meditate over the psalms and begin writing your song. Singing your new song out loud to the Lord can be the gift from your heart to the heart of your heavenly Father.

Action Steps I Can Take Today

It is important that we learn to say "thank you" and to express our gratitude to God. It's also important that we do the same to people. When the Philippians read Paul's letter, they were probably filled anew with joy and an even greater desire to help Paul and others in the future. When others bless our lives, we need to encourage them by expressing our gratitude. It will strengthen them and uplift us.

Ask God to show you if there is someone to whom you need to express love and gratitude today. (It might be the person or persons who shared the gospel with you.) Determine to act upon what God reveals to you. Let Him guide you to write a note or email, make a phone call or meet in person with the individual. Let your attitude be one of gratitude.

THREE

OVERCOME WORRY

In a sense, this lesson is a continuation of chapter 2. Paul's greatest desire for the Philippian believers was that they "rejoice in the Lord always" (Philippians 4:4). But we can't experience joy, nor can we fully rejoice, when our heart is laden down with worries. Worries have the power to destroy our peace, our contentment and our joy.

Is worry robbing you of experiencing all that God has for you? In this chapter, you'll see how Paul's trust in the Lord enabled him to face an uncertain future without worrying. If you will follow his example, you, too, can learn the secret of overcoming worry.

A Closer Look at the Problem

Before you begin this week's study, ask God to show you specific areas where worry is robbing you of contentment. Draw an outline of a heart in your journal and divide it into sections. Label each section with a specific person or situation you're worried about right now. Ask God to reveal to your mind and heart His way of overcoming each worry as you work through this lesson. Probably we Christians worry most about the people we love. We want them to be happy and well and in a right relationship with God.

Read Philippians 1:3-6. What was Paul's attitude as he prayed (see verses 3-4)?

_____

_____

_____

_____

What reasons did Paul give for his joy and gratitude (see verse 6)?

_____

_____

_____

_____

What do you think would have happened to Paul's joy if he had spent his time worrying about how the Lord was working in these people?

_____

_____

_____

_____

Paul loved the Philippians, and it would have been easy for him to worry about them. However, his confidence was not in the Philippians but in God's great power to work in their lives. When our confidence is in people and their power to stay strong in the Lord, we have reason to worry. But when we put our confidence in God's power to work in their lives, His comforting presence will give us peace.

A Closer Look at God's Truth

Read Philippians 2:13. According to this verse, what is God doing?

_____

_____

_____

_____

What are some ways that God works in you to will and to work for His good pleasure?

_____

_____

_____

_____

Write Philippians 2:13 in your own words, making it applicable to you personally. Then reword it to apply to someone whom you worry about.

_____

_____

_____

_____

God wants us and those we love to grow. We don't always recognize the hand of God in difficult situations, but we need to trust that God is working to make our lives pleasing to Him. He is also concerned about the ones we love and is working in their lives as well. Read Philippians 1:19-20. What indications do you have from these two verses that Paul was not worried, even though he was in prison and faced an uncertain future?

_____

_____

_____

_____

List several things that Paul expected to happen.

_____

_____

_____

_____

Why did he expect these results?

_____

_____

_____

_____

What effect did these expectations have on Paul's outlook in life?

_____

_____

_____

_____

In these verses, Paul expressed what he expected from God. This process of affirmation is important in overcoming worry and other harmful attitudes. When we find ourselves worrying, we need to find promises in God's Word, and then, if we are fulfilling the requirements, we need to claim those promises aloud. As we claim God's promises, our faith grows and our fears shrink. Read Philippians 3:3. What did Paul say he would not put his confidence in?

_____

_____

_____

_____

What was Paul trusting in instead?

_____

_____

_____

What dangers are there in putting confidence in the flesh?

_____

_____

_____

_____

The flesh is the old nature that cries out to us to do things in our own strength, in our own way. Paul realized that neither he nor anyone else could find peace with God through his own works. He knew that he had to put his confidence in God for growth and salvation in his own life as well as in the lives of others. Read Jeremiah 17:5-8. What does God say about the person who trusts in mankind and in his own strength (see verse 5)?

_____

_____

_____

_____

What does trusting in ourselves show about our relationship with God?

_____

_____

_____

_____

How is the person who trusts self, or the flesh, described in verse 6?

_____

_____

_____

_____

How does verse 6 relate to a person's spiritual life?

_____

_____

_____

How is the person who trusts in the Lord described (see verses 7-8)?

_____

_____

_____

_____

To what is such a person compared (see verse 8)?

_____

_____

_____

_____

What phrases in verse 8 imply a time of problems or difficulties?

_____

_____

_____

_____

What is promised during times of trial (see verse 8)?

_____

_____

_____

_____

What is the condition of these promises (see verse 7)?

_____

_____

_____

_____

_____

This passage shows clearly that if we trust in ourselves or in other people, the end result will be a life that is unfruitful. When we put our trust in the Lord, a fruitful and productive life results. Even in times of difficulties, we will not have to be anxious or fearful. Any time we begin to fear or worry, we need to recognize those emotions as a signal that we are not trusting God. We have either begun to trust ourselves or have begun to doubt God's power or willingness to work in a situation. Read Matthew 6:25-34. In verses 25 and 26, Jesus said not to worry about our lives—what we eat, drink or wear. What reasons did He give for not worrying?

_____

_____

_____

Reword verse 26 to make it Jesus' personal message to you.

_____

_____

_____

What does worrying accomplish (see verse 27)?

_____

_____

_____

Why did Jesus say we shouldn't worry about what we're going to wear (see verses 28-30)?

_____

_____

_____

What command did Jesus give (see verse 31)?

_____

_____

_____

_____

What did Jesus say causes worrying (see verse 30)?

_____

_____

_____

_____

What reason did Jesus give for not worrying (see verse 32)?

_____

_____

_____

When Jesus referred to the Gentiles, He was referring to those who did not believe in God. They did not know a heavenly Father that they could trust to take care of them. We, however, have a Father who knows exactly what we need. According to verse 33, what command did Jesus give? What promise?

_____

_____

_____

What did Jesus tell us not to worry about (see verse 34)?

_____

_____

_____

What happens to today's contentment when we worry about tomorrow?

_____

_____

_____

Jesus encouraged His listeners to trust a loving, caring heavenly Father who even takes care of birds and grasses. He encouraged them to make God's kingdom and His righteousness their top priority. When Jesus spoke of God's kingdom, He was referring to that realm where God is King. When we seek God's kingdom and His righteousness, we are seeking to make God the King and Ruler of our lives. When that becomes our number one priority, God promises to take care of everything else. Paul had done that in his life (see Philippians 1:20-21). As a result, he had assurance that God would take care of him. He saw no reason to worry.

Reread Philippians 2:17-18. What was Paul's attitude, even though he realized that his life might be taken from him?

_____

_____

_____

Read Philippians 1:21. Paul said, "For to me, to live is _____ and to die is _____." Paul was able to face such difficult circumstances without worry because he felt that whether he lived or died, he would come out a winner. Because Paul didn't worry about what tomorrow held, he could rejoice daily knowing that His faithful God was in control. Paul expressed his joy for today, even though tomorrow threatened to be difficult. He also encouraged the Philippians to rejoice with him regardless of their circumstances. Paul knew for sure that worrying about what the future holds does absolutely no good; it simply robs us of today's joys.

Read Philippians 1:27-30. What phrases in these verses indicate that the Philippians were also experiencing some difficult times?

_____

_____

_____

_____

What did Paul say was his desire for them (see verse 27-28)?

_____

_____

_____

What attitude did Paul discourage (see verse 28)?

_____

_____

_____

How did Paul encourage the Philippians to look at the opposition and the suffering (see verse 29)?

_____

_____

_____

_____

Paul indicated that the Philippians had been given the privilege of suffering for Jesus (see verse 29). How would that attitude affect a person facing an uncertain future?

_____

_____

_____

_____

Can you think of any reasons why a person suffering for Christ would be blessed?

_____

_____

_____

_____

Usually a person will not suffer for Christ unless he or she has a close relationship with God. The individual with this close relationship will experience far greater joys and blessings than those who are not totally committed to Christ. The person who has a close relationship with God will not have to worry about future suffering because he or she trusts God to sustain and strengthen him or her through it. Read Philippians 4:6-7. What was Paul's command about worrying in verse 6?

_____

_____

_____

_____

Instead of worry, what attitude should accompany the Philippians' prayers?

_____

_____

_____

_____

Why do you think Paul encouraged the Philippians to pray with thanksgiving about things that could worry them?

_____

_____

_____

_____

What part should thanksgiving have in your prayer life?

_____

_____

_____

_____

What will be the result?

_____

_____

_____

_____

_____

How is God's peace described?

_____

_____

_____

_____

A Closer Look at My Own Heart

In this study on overcoming worry, we have discovered that peace is the opposite of worry. We've also discovered the power of thanksgiving.

When we pray about problems with an attitude of thanksgiving, God somehow takes those problems and begins to work miracles. The first miracle is His peace. When we worry, we open a door for Satan to steal our joy. If we pray instead, God shuts that door, and His peace will guard our hearts and minds in Christ Jesus (see Philippians 4:7). When we thank God for the results we do not see, then God gives us faith to claim His promises before they are a reality. Trusting God to work gives us peace in place of anxiety.

Read Isaiah 26:3-4. What are the conditions for finding peace?

_____

_____

_____

What reason is given for trusting in God?

_____

_____

_____

In the *New King James Version*, Isaiah 26:3 reads, "You [God] will keep him in perfect peace, whose mind is stayed on You." Worrying is an indication that we have shifted the focus of our minds onto our problem and away from

God, the problem solver. If by an act of will we determine to focus on God and His strength rather than on our problem, God will give us His peace.

You can begin to do that right now by taking out the heart diagram you made earlier (see the first page of this chapter). Look at it, and then determine to give God the worries you listed there. Write "To God" at the top and "From [your name]" at the bottom. Write Isaiah 26:3-4 underneath it and then draw an outline of a rock around the entire heart.

How do you feel knowing that you have—in the best way you know how—given your worries to your Father?

_____

_____

_____

_____

Action Steps I Can Take Today

Even though God has called us to trust Him, there are times when we simply do not know how to make this a reality. We want to trust, but somehow, we can't. Mark 9:24 is the account of another person who had difficulty believing, crying out, "I do believe; help my unbelief."

God knows the struggle you are going through and He wants to help. Ask Him for greater faith to believe and to trust that He will take care of your problems. Then thank Him for what He is going to do in your life.

Read Mark 5:21-24,35-36. What did Jesus say to Jairus (verse 36)?

_____

_____

_____

_____

_____

What is Jesus saying to you?

_____

_____

_____

_____

_____

Jesus does not want fear to rob us of the joy and peace that He came to give. Write Isaiah 26:3-4 on a small index card. On the back write the following prayer:

> *Lord, I admit that I don't know how to trust and that I know*
> *that worrying is a sin. You have promised that if I confess my sins,*
> *You will forgive and cleanse me. Right now, I claim that promise of for-*
> *giveness and cleansing, and I ask You to fill me with Your faith. I ask You*
> *to help my unbelief and teach me to focus on You and Your power.*
> *Thank You in Jesus' name for the victory that is mine.*

Review your index card every day this week.

FOUR

RENEW YOUR MIND

We live in a negative world. Newscasters update us on the bad things that are happening around us. The media show us what we lack to experience "the good life": the perfect body build, the biggest house with the latest gadgets, a vacation in an exotic locale. Our mind taunts us, *Why not me?* Even employees and employers can't seem to find anything good to say about each other—or even about themselves.

This constant barrage of negatives can rob us of peace and destroy our contentment. And that isn't all. We all have within us a propensity toward the dark side. Paul wrote, "For our struggle is not against flesh and blood, but against the rulers, against the powers, against the world forces of this darkness" (Ephesians 6:12).

Although we can't remove all the negatives from our lives, we can guard ourselves against allowing them to control us. This chapter shows us how.

A Closer Look at the Problem

Part of the reason Paul was content in all circumstances is that he had allowed God to transform his mind. This enabled him to experience peace and contentment. As we learn to change our thought patterns from dwelling on negative circumstances to focusing on the blessing of God, we too will experience the peace and contentment Paul knew so well.

Paul realized that the way a person thinks affects the way he or she feels and acts. A person who concentrates on the blessings of God will rejoice and experience God's peace. If, instead, a person dwells on everything that goes wrong, he or she will be filled with anger, bitterness, fear, hate and a multitude of other negative emotions. No one can experience those emotions and be content. Paul desired that the Philippians share the contentment and joy he knew, so he encouraged them to focus on positive things.

Read Philippians 4:8-9. List the things that Paul encouraged the Philippians to think about.

_____

_____

_____

What effect would the following things have on a person's worry?

Anger

_____

_____

_____

Resentment

_____

_____

_____

Hatred

_____

_____

_____

Do you think letting your mind dwell only on good things will help to bring peace and contentment? Why or why not?

_____

_____

_____

A Closer Look at God's Truth

Focusing on Jesus renews our mind and gives us His perspective on how to deal with negatives; only then can we have true contentment. Read Philippians 1:12-18. According to verses 12-14, what did Paul choose to let his mind dwell on?

_____

_____

_____

What adversities could Paul have thought about instead?

_____

_____

_____

What do you think happened in Paul's life as a result of his choice of focus?

_____

_____

_____

According to verses 15-18, what positive fact did Paul choose to think about?

_____

_____

_____

What emotions could Paul have experienced if he had focused on the negative things in his life?

_____

_____

_____

What emotions did Paul experience as a result of thinking about the positive things in his life?

_____

_____

_____

Many people are robbed of joy when they allow their minds to dwell on some painful thing that another person has said or done. (Whether the hurt was intentional or accidental does not seem to matter much.)

Paul could have felt that way about the people who were preaching to "stir up trouble for" him (verse 17). Had those negative feelings been his point of focus, he could not have rejoiced at the spread of the gospel. He probably would have become angry and resentful, and His joy in the Lord would have disappeared. Instead, he chose to focus on the fact that the gospel was being preached and people were coming to know Jesus as their personal Savior. With his mind dwelling on that fact, he could rejoice and be content.

Read Ephesians 4:26-27. What do these verses teach us about anger?

_____

_____

_____

Relate Ephesians 4:26 to refusing to dwell on what makes you angry.

_____

_____

_____

By setting a time limit (such as sunset), Paul ensured that anger would be dealt with—gotten rid of—daily so that none of it could carry over to the next day. What are some hurtful situations that you sometimes choose to let your mind dwell upon? How do these affect your relationships at home?

_____

_____

_____

How do these affect your relationships at church?

_____

_____

_____

How do these affect your relationships at work?

_____

_____

_____

In Hebrews 12:14-15, we are encouraged to pursue peace, not anger. The implication in these verses is that an unforgiving spirit results in bitterness. How does forgiveness or lack of forgiveness affect peace and contentment?

_____

_____

_____

How can bitterness make many defiled?

_____

_____

_____

Read Matthew 5:44. How did Jesus say we should treat those who mistreat us?

_____

_____

_____

Read Matthew 6:14-15. Why is forgiveness so important in the life of the Christian?

_____

_____

_____

Jesus asked us to pray for those who have hurt or misused us. When we obey His command, even though we don't always feel like obeying it, God will give us His grace to love and forgive the person who mistreated us. However, we need to realize that even though we choose to forgive and pray for that person, the emotion of love may not immediately follow. Often the healing of wounds takes time. Read Philippians 1:19-26. What did Paul choose to make the focus of his thoughts (see verse 19)?

_____

_____

_____

What positive aspects of death did Paul choose to think about?

_____

_____

_____

What positive aspects of living did Paul choose to focus on (see verses 20-22, 24-26)?

_____

_____

_____

What effect do you think Paul's focus had on his attitude as he sat in prison, not knowing what the future held?

_____

_____

_____

Though he faced an uncertain future, Paul did not focus on all that could go wrong. He focused on Jesus Christ and the eternal reward that would be his. Often when we look at the future, we tend to magnify everything that could go wrong. That becomes our focus and instead of peace, we experience fear and frustration. In order to find peace and contentment, we need to learn to focus on Jesus Christ and the good He can bring into the future rather than on the bad things that might happen.

Read Philippians 2:5 from several different Bible translations. What did Paul desire for the Philippians?

_____
_____
_____
_____
_____

If the Philippians had this attitude, how would the following have been affected?

Their minds

_____
_____
_____

Their doubts

_____
_____
_____

Their forgiveness

_____
_____
_____

Their fears

_____
_____
_____

Their anger

_____

_____

_____

Their frustrations

_____

_____

_____

Their outlook in general

_____

_____

_____

Because Paul's desire was that the Philippians have the same mind and the same attitude that Christ had, we can know that it is God's will for us to have them too. However, this isn't always easy. Read 2 Corinthians 10:3-5. What kind of battle is described in these verses?

_____

_____

_____

What kind of weapons must be used (see verse 4)?

_____

_____

_____

What did Paul expect to happen as a result of this warfare (see verse 5)?

_____

_____

_____

What kind of fortresses, or strongholds, do you think Paul was talking about in verse 4?

_____

_____

_____

How are the fortresses destroyed (see verse 5)?

_____

_____

_____

What must be done with every thought (see verse 5)?

_____

_____

_____

_____

There is often a battle going on in our mind that requires the kind of warfare that Paul described in these verses. Satan desires to build fortresses of anger, bitterness, pride, self-pity and a multitude of other negative emotions in our minds. He knows that those emotions will keep us spiritually ineffective and emotionally discontent.

For us to gain victory in Christ, we must make these negative thoughts subject to the obedience of Jesus Christ. He has the power to change those thoughts if we are willing to let Him. When we experience a negative thought, we must bring that thought to Him and ask Him to overcome it. As we ask Him to replace our negative thoughts with His attitudes, we will demolish fortresses and gain victory over them.

Read Ephesians 6:11-18. Why is it necessary to prepare our minds with God's truth (see verses 11-13)?

_____

_____

_____

With what are we to clothe ourselves (see verses 14-17)?

_____

_____

_____

What additional actions are suggested in verse 18?

_____

_____

_____

Why is the mind so important in a Christian's battle against Satan?

_____

_____

_____

How do you think a Christian clothes his or her mind with truth?

_____

_____

_____

_____

Read Romans 12:1-3. What did Paul urge the Romans to do (see verse 1)?

_____

_____

_____

What kind of sacrifice is acceptable to God (see verse 1)?

_____

_____

_____

_____

What were the Romans commanded not to do (see verse 2)?

_____

_____

_____

_____

What were they to do instead (see verse 2)?

_____

_____

_____

How did Paul say they would be transformed (see verse 3)?

_____

_____

_____

_____

What steps do you feel a Christian needs to take in order to renew his or her mind?

_____

_____

_____

_____

_____

Rewrite verse 2 in your own words. Make it applicable to you personally.

_____

_____

_____

_____

Read Ephesians 4:17-24. How did Paul describe the unbeliever's mind in verses 17-19?

_____

_____

_____

_____

What is the result of the condition of the unbeliever's mind (see verse 18)?

_____

_____

_____

_____

Where is truth to be found (see verse 21)?

_____

_____

_____

_____

What is necessary before we can put on the new self (see verses 22-23)?

_____

_____

_____

_____

How is the new self described (see verse 24)?

_____

_____

_____

What do you think Paul meant by his description of the new self in verse 24?

_____

_____

_____

How is a renewed mind related to the new self described in verse 24?

_____

_____

_____

When a person accepts Christ as Savior, he or she experiences a new birth. Although that person now desires to serve the Lord, the old human nature is still within him or her (see Mark 7:21-23). This results in a fierce struggle between the two natures, the old and the new.

As we allow Christ to renew our minds, our spiritual nature grows stronger and we become more and more Christlike. However, even though we're Christians, we frequently commit sinful actions in our lives. When we desperately try to change those actions and bring our lives into conformity with Christ, we often fail and give up in frustration. We need to understand that the renewal of our mind is an ongoing process that must take place *daily*. When God's thoughts become part of our thoughts, our attitudes and emotions will be right. When our thinking is in line with God's thinking, the actions in our lives will also be in harmony with God's will and His purpose for us.

A Closer Look at My Own Heart

Read John 5:5-9. In this thought-provoking story, Jesus asked a man who was paralyzed for 38 years if he wanted to be made well. Why do you think Jesus asked him that question?

_____

_____

_____

Why would a person want to be sick?

_____
_____
_____
_____
_____

Do you think the man's desire to be well was necessary for Jesus to heal him?

_____
_____
_____
_____
_____

What did Jesus command him to do (see verse 8)?

_____
_____
_____
_____

How did the man respond (see verse 9)?

_____
_____
_____
_____

Before Jesus could heal this man, the man had to desire wholeness. The same is true with your emotions. You must desire God's contentment, joy and peace, or you will focus on the wrong things. Initially, you would probably think, *Of course, I want to be content,* but then you choose to let your mind dwell on what makes you unhappy.

Jesus commanded the paralyzed man to arise and walk. In the same way, Jesus commands you to set aside self-pity and despair and to walk in the hope of Jesus Christ. You have a choice. You must truthfully answer Jesus' question, "Do you want to be well?"

The only way you can develop a Christlike mind is to put the thoughts of Christ into your mind. His thoughts are found in the Word of God. As you memorize verses, personalize them and speak them aloud, God's thoughts and attitudes will influence your thoughts and attitudes. Your life will be transformed. You will reflect the power and love of Jesus Christ.

Read Joshua 1:8 and Psalm 1:1-3. According to these verses, what are you to do with God's Word?

_____

_____

_____

_____

What effect will meditating on God's Word have on your actions?

_____

_____

_____

_____

What is promised to you when you meditate upon God's Word?

_____

_____

_____

_____

Action Steps I Can Take Today

Is there an area of weakness in your life that you need to let God transform? Describe that area.

_____

_____

_____

_____

Find a Scripture verse that promises victory for your weakness, and then personalize the verse and memorize it. Meditate upon that promise. For example:

- If you have a struggle with controlling your mouth, you could personalize Philippians 4:13: "I can control my mouth through Christ who strengthens me."

- If you have a problem with fear, you could memorize and personalize 2 Timothy 1:7: "God has not given me a spirit of timidity [fear (*KJV*)] but of power and love and discipline."

- If you struggle with guilt, you could memorize and personalize 1 John 1:9: "Since I have confessed my sin, God is faithful and righteous to forgive and to cleanse me from all unrighteousness."

Is there someone with whom you can be accountable concerning this area—someone with whom you can share your weakness and your verse? Ask that person if he or she will pray for you each day this week.

FIVE

APPROPRIATE CHRIST'S RIGHTEOUSNESS

Nancy was what many would describe as a fireball Christian. She led a women's Bible study in her community and helped spearhead an organization to help the homeless. Whenever her children's schoolteachers needed something, they called Nancy. It was the same at church. Nancy organized socials and served on committees. She also served on the worship team and substituted in the Sunday School Department.

But instead of feeling joy and contentment, Nancy felt used and angry. She almost wanted to drop out of everything. But if she wasn't there, how would anything get done? Besides, her friends were always telling her what a great job she was doing. So why was Nancy discontent?

In this chapter, we'll examine why depending on our on strengths, abilities or good works will not lead to contentment. No matter what we do on our own, we will always be unhappy. Instead, we must choose to appropriate Christ's righteousness, trusting God's grace to give us power and contentment.

A Closer Look at the Problem

According to the religious standards of his day, Paul had accomplished a great deal for God. However, he knew he could never gain Christ's righteousness through any of his own works. Paul's example is a constant reminder that no matter how impressive our spiritual accomplishments may be, they are worthless if we think they gain us any righteousness. It is only as we appropriate Christ's righteousness that we are made right in God's sight.

The verb "appropriate" may be a difficult word for some people to grasp. In its simplest form, however, it means to take for one's own. Just as non-Christians must realize they are powerless to save themselves, Christians must realize that in their own strength and abilities, they cannot effectively serve God.

As long as we depend on what we can do in our own strength, we cannot appropriate the power of the eternal God. We struggle in our weaknesses because we are trusting our works instead of God's grace. When we depend on God's grace, we have the same power available to us that raised Christ from the dead.

What are some outward actions that people trust in to make them right with God?

_____
_____
_____
_____

What dangers are involved in trusting our good works?

_____
_____
_____
_____

What are some of the ways you have tried to gain God's favor—either before you were a Christian or after you trusted Christ?

_____
_____
_____
_____
_____

A Closer Look at God's Truth

One of the reasons Paul wrote to the Philippians was to warn them about false teachers who had come into the church and were teaching that circumcision was necessary for a man to become a Christian.

Circumcision had been instituted by God as a symbol of the covenant between Himself and Abraham. It was a sign that Abraham's descendants were a people set apart by God as His own. Down through the generations, all Jewish males were circumcised as a symbol that they belonged to God (see Genesis 17:9-14). If a Gentile wished to join the Jewish faith, he was required to submit to circumcision.

During Paul's time, some Jewish teachers in the Church were teaching that in order to become a follower of Jesus, a man needed to be circumcised and follow all the Jewish laws.

Read Philippians 3:2-3 and 2 Peter 2:1. What terms did Paul use to describe anyone who would lead someone astray with false teachings?

_____

_____

_____

_____

_____

How did Paul describe "the true circumcision" (Philippians 3:3)?

_____

_____

_____

_____

_____

Jeremiah 9:25-26 gives us insight on what Paul meant by this phrase. In these verses, the Lord declared that He would punish all who were circumcised (ceremonially clean) yet were uncircumcised (unclean in their hearts). According to this passage, what does the Lord desire: outward acts of righteousness (good works) alone or outward acts of righteousness combined with right motives and right relationship with God?

_____

_____

_____

_____

_____

Read Philippians 3:4-6. How did Paul describe his works in comparison to the works of others (see verse 4)?

_____

_____

_____

_____

_____

List all the advantages that Paul had in being right with God, according to Jewish law (see verses 5-6).

_____

_____

_____

_____

_____

What was his condition according to the Jewish way of thinking (see verse 6)?

_____

_____

_____

_____

_____

Read Philippians 3:7-9. What terms did Paul use to describe the way he felt about his works?

_____

_____

_____

_____

The Greek word that is translated "rubbish" in verse 8 refers to what is thrown away or rejected as worthless. It included such filth as the waste of slaughtered animals. This is the way that Paul had begun to look at his works. While he was trusting in himself, those works were keeping him from trusting God. In that way, they were a hindrance to him. They were worse than nothing because they kept him from acknowledging a need for Jesus.

Just as Paul regarded his works as garbage, we must also throw out all reliance on our works as a way of becoming right with God. What reason did Paul give for counting these things "as loss" (see verse 7)?

_____

_____

_____

_____

What things must we be willing to treat as garbage, or rubbish, in order to gain Christ?

_____

_____

_____

_____

Why is this necessary?

_____

_____

_____

_____

What did Paul gain by accepting Christ and counting all works as rubbish (see verse 9)?

_____

_____

_____

Write a description of the kind of righteousness Paul had before he trusted Christ (see also Isaiah 64:6).

_____

_____

_____

_____

Jesus came to this earth and lived a perfect life. He had no sin. Then He willingly gave His life as the perfect sacrifice to pay the penalty for sin. He came to bridge the gap between a holy God and sinful humankind. Our sins have separated us from God, but by accepting Christ's righteousness, we are brought into a right relationship with God.

Paul was ready to throw everything away in order to gain Christ and His righteousness. Paul was willing to throw away his dependence upon his works, his position, his family and his wealth. He gave them all up to gain eternal and abundant life through Jesus Christ. As a result, Jesus took Paul's sin and exchanged that sin for His righteousness. In God's eyes, Paul became the righteousness of Jesus. God no longer saw Paul as sinful; He looked at Paul and saw Jesus' righteousness instead.

What about you? When God looks at you, what does He see?

_____

_____

_____

_____

Read Philippians 3:10-11. What are the results of accepting Christ's righteousness?

_____

_____

_____

_____

Paul said that one of the benefits of accepting Christ's righteousness is knowing "the power of His resurrection" (Philippians 3:10). What do you think Paul meant by that phrase (see also Ephesians 1:18-20)?

_____

_____

_____

_____

Why is it necessary for us to consider our works as worthless in order to experience Christ's power?

_____

_____

_____

In Philippians 3:10, Paul also speaks of knowing "the fellowship of His suffering." What do you think Paul was talking about?

_____

_____

_____

In 2 Corinthians 12:7-10, Paul described a difficult condition he experienced. He called it "a thorn in the flesh" (verse 7). He said that God had allowed this, even though he had asked Him three times to remove it. How is Paul's reaction, described in verse 9, an example of Christ's power being glorified through Paul's weaknesses?

_____

_____

_____

_____

Why do you think God's power is perfected in weakness?

_____

_____

_____

_____

_____

What part does realizing our weaknesses play in accepting God's grace?

_____

_____

_____

_____

How is realizing our weaknesses an example of the fellowship of suffering?

_____

_____

_____

_____

_____

There are times in our Christian life when we go through periods of suffering and testing. Paul also went through such times. We need to realize that as we live the Christian life, there *will be* difficult times. However, God wants to use those times to strengthen us and to bring greater spiritual growth and increased ministry into our lives (see James 1:2-4).

God's grace is the love and favor He freely gives us, even though we have done nothing to deserve it. When we Christians go through times of suffering, there are two ways we can react: (1) We can reject God's grace and become bitter, or (2) we can let God's grace comfort us and make us better. If we can recognize that even in a difficult situation, God is going to work for our good, then God's grace and love will comfort us and bring us peace. He can use our weaknesses and our suffering to draw us closer to His side and to bring glory to Himself.

When Paul spoke of "the fellowship of His sufferings," he recognized that when a Christian suffers for Christ, God pours out an abundance of His grace to comfort that person. If we will accept God's grace at that point, we will grow in the Lord and experience His peace and joy instead of bitterness and anger.

Reread Philippians 3:10. What does it mean for a person to become like Jesus in His death?

_____

_____

_____

_____

_____

What is the result of being conformed to His death?

_____

_____

_____

_____

_____

Paul's letter to the Roman Christians helps us understand what being conformed to His death means. Read Romans 6:1-14. In what ways are we to be conformed to His death?

_____

_____

_____

_____

_____

What are the results of putting the old self to death?

_____

_____

_____

_____

_____

In what ways does a Christian experience resurrection with Jesus?

_____

_____

_____

_____

What is necessary to experience that resurrection?

_____

_____

_____

_____

When Paul told of the benefits of having a righteousness based on faith in Christ rather than in his own works, one of those benefits was that he might be conformed to Christ's death. Just as Christ had to put to death His own natural desires to live and to exalt Himself, so we must also put to death our natural desires to sin and be in control of self. But we need to remember that until we see our righteousness as worthless and accept Christ's righteousness, we can never put that old sinful nature to death. Unless we, through Christ's power, crucify the old sinful nature, we cannot experience the resurrection to new life in Christ.

Read Philippians 1:2. What was Paul's desire for the Philippians?

_____

_____

_____

Who is the source of these blessings?

_____

_____

_____

_____

Which blessing comes first?

_____

_____

_____

_____

Why is it necessary to accept God's grace before we can experience God's peace?

_____

_____

_____

_____

A Closer Look at My Own Heart

At the beginning of this study, we looked at the life of a young woman named Nancy. Perhaps you saw a bit of yourself in her—a driven woman, a tired woman, a woman so busy doing all she can do that she lost her contentment and joy. What about you? In what ways can you identify with Nancy?

_____

_____

_____

_____

Read the word picture in John 15:4-8. In this word picture, who is the vine?

_____

_____

_____

_____

Who are the branches?

_____

_____

_____

_____

In verse 5, what did Jesus promise to do?

_____

_____

_____

_____

Now ask yourself, *Have I ever seen a branch by itself bear fruit?* Of course you haven't. A branch bears fruit because it is connected to the vine. It is only from the vine that it receives power to produce fruit. How would an understanding of this principle change Nancy's life?

_____

_____

_____

How can it change yours?

_____

_____

_____

_____

When a Christian tries to bear fruit in his or her own strength, he or she will begin to focus on his or her own works instead of on God's power. Then he or she will either become proud because of personal good works or become discouraged because of failure. Either way, God cannot use that person the way He would like to.

If we will realize that our works will never make us right with God, we can get our eyes off what we can do in our own strength and begin to rely on Jesus. He is the author and finisher of our faith. He is the only One who can bring us to our full potential so that we can experience true contentment.

Action Steps I Can Take Today

Read through the following questions. Choose the one that best describes the prayer you most need to pray right now, and then have a private conversation with God.

1. Is there an area of suffering in your life in which you need to accept God's grace and power to enable you to overcome bitterness and anger? Tell God about it, and then open your heart to receive His grace.

2. Is there some area of weakness that you need to praise God for because He can be exalted through it? Acknowledge that weakness. Thank God for it. Ask Him for His strength and grace and believe that you will receive it.

3. Are you trying to make yourself right with God through your works? Acknowledge that your works cannot make you right with God. Ask God to forgive and cleanse you of all unrighteousness.

4. Are you struggling to live the Christian life in your own strength? Pray the following prayer—it will help you acknowledge your weaknesses and open yourself up to His power.

Lord, I acknowledge that I can never be right with You through my works. I acknowledge that I am weak and helpless in my strength. I accept Your strength and Your grace to empower me to live for You. I accept the righteousness of Christ for my own and I praise You, God, for exchanging my sin and weaknesses for Jesus' righteousness and power.

$\mathcal{F}$ORGET THE PAST

In the last chapter, we learned that once Paul stopped trusting in his own works, he could forget the past with its failures and disappointments and move forward in a growing relationship with Jesus Christ. If we are to find true contentment, we must do the same thing.

But how do we move forward with Jesus Christ? How do we deal with guilt over past sins and failures? How do we accept the fact that we need to seek forgiveness from any person we've hurt? How do we deal with unresolved anger? This chapter will help us discover how we can dismantle roadblocks and begin to move forward in our Christian walk.

A Closer Look at the Problem

Consider the following scenarios:

Mary slept with a lot of men before she became a Christian. Now she has met a Christian man who truly loves her and wants to marry her. But guilt over her previous relationships won't let her say yes to this young man. How can Mary be free of this guilt?

Paula, an older woman, has turned a lot of her friends away from God by harboring an intensely critical spirit. But instead of going to these people and asking for forgiveness, she makes excuses for herself: "Well, everybody has their faults. Nobody's perfect."

Rene's husband, Tom, has a tendency to put things off. "I'll take care of that tomorrow," he says, but tomorrow comes and he doesn't do it. Instead of talking to her husband about how she feels, Rene lets resentment grow inside her. Resentment turns to anger, anger to bitterness. Rene wishes now that she had never married Tom.

Each of these women is facing a roadblock that is keeping her from growing in her relationship with Jesus Christ. All three roadblocks are rooted in the past. What effect does your past have upon you?

_____

_____

_____

_____

What things in your past must you be willing to deal with and forget?

_____

_____

_____

_____

What will happen if you continue to dwell upon the past?

_____

_____

_____

_____

A Closer Look at God's Truth

Read Philippians 3:7-17. What did Paul desire for his life (see verses 8-10)?

_____

_____

_____

_____

What was his ultimate goal (see verse 11)?

_____

_____

_____

Did Paul feel that he had obtained perfection (see verse 12)? Why or why not?

_____

_____

_____

_____

The Greek word translated in verse 12 as "perfect" can also mean finished or complete. So Paul was saying that he was not a totally finished and complete Christian. In Christ, he had Jesus' righteousness, but as a human he still had areas that needed God's polishing. What did Paul say he was doing because he had not yet obtained perfection (see verse 12)?

_____

_____

_____

_____

Why was Paul doing this?

_____

_____

_____

_____

Read verses 12-14 in several different Bible translations. What do you think Paul meant when he said, "I press on so that I may lay hold of that for which also I was laid hold of by Christ Jesus" (verse 12)?

_____

_____

_____

What was Paul's objective (see verses 13-14)?

_____

_____

_____

In this passage, Paul was referring to athletes in a race. Unlike in modern times, where a string is stretched across the finish line, during Paul's time a finishing post marked the end of the race. The athlete who reached the post first grabbed hold of it, winning the prize. Likewise, Paul was pressing on to his finishing point. He wanted to lay hold of the prize—resurrection to a new, sinless, glorified body and life eternally with Jesus.

When Paul wrote that he was laid hold of by Christ, he meant that Jesus had reached down and taken hold of him so that he could take hold of the resurrection available through Jesus. What two things were necessary for Paul to achieve his objective (see verse 13)?

_____

_____

_____

Why do you think it was necessary for Paul to forget the past in order to "press on toward the goal for the prize of the upward call of God" (verse 14)?

_____

_____

_____

RESOLVING GUILT FROM THE PAST

Guilt from past sins or failures often keeps a Christian looking backward. Unfortunately, when a person concentrates on the past, he or she is more likely to repeat it. Fearing more sins and failures and feeling not good enough to serve God, the person is hindered in his or her growth and ministry.

According to Acts 26:9-11, what things did Paul need to forget?

_____

_____

_____

How would Paul's ministry have been affected had he dwelt on those things?

_____

_____

_____

_____

Read Psalm 32:3-4. List the results of feeling guilty about the past.

_____

_____

_____

These verses in Psalm 32 show the devastating effect of guilt upon Christians. That is why before we can move ahead in Christ, we must deal with our sins and failures. We also need to realize that one of Satan's most effective weapons against us is guilt. Satan reminds us of our past failures and tries to deceive us into believing that God could not or would not forgive us for such terrible sins. Just as Satan was overcome by the blood of the Lamb and the testimony of the saints, we can overcome Satan's attacks by using God's weapons (see Revelation 12:10-11). We need to claim the forgiveness that is ours because of Jesus' death (see 1 John 1:8-10).

SEEKING FORGIVENESS FROM OTHERS

Sometimes we find it difficult to leave the past behind because we haven't obeyed Christ's command to go to a person we have hurt and ask the person for forgiveness.

Read Matthew 5:23-24. What did Jesus command us to do?

_____

_____

_____

Why do you think God commanded this?

_____

_____

_____

Have you ever asked another person to forgive you? How did you feel before and after?

_____

_____

_____

How did seeking the forgiveness affect your relationship with God?

_____

_____

_____

How was your relationship with the other person affected?

_____

_____

_____

In some cases, asking for forgiveness means making restitution. This is often very difficult to do, but the release of guilt we experience and the love that God gives for the other person are tremendous. Even in situations in which we have been only partly to blame, we still need to ask forgiveness for that part, however small it may have been. If we do not do this, every time we see that person or hear his or her name, we will remember our guilt and the hurt we caused.

We also need to remember that in some situations, forgiveness might not be immediately granted to us. Hurts that go deep may take time to heal before reconciliation can take place. The point is that no matter what, we must seek forgiveness from people we've hurt. Otherwise, we will not be able to forget the past and press forward in Christ.

Read Psalm 32:5-7. What are the results of forgiveness?

DEALING WITH UNRESOLVED ANGER

Another area that often must be dealt with in order to forget the past is unresolved anger. Anger over something that has happened to us or to those we love can result in bitterness, hatred and unforgiveness. Many Christians feel that it is a sin to be angry, and they deny their anger. This can have devastating results on our bodies and on our relationships with others. Anger in itself is not sin—even Jesus got angry. But the way we deal with anger can be a sin, thus creating another roadblock. If we stuff our anger inside and try to pretend it isn't there, we will be unable to forget the past and move ahead in Christ.

Read Matthew 18:15-17. Who is the first person you should talk to if someone has sinned against you (see verse 15)?

What will be the result if that person listens?

Why do you think Jesus commanded us to first go privately to the person who has sinned against us?

_____

_____

_____

It's important to be careful that while expressing your anger, you do not bring an uninvolved person into the picture and leave that individual carrying your wrath. When you tell a person how someone has mistreated you, the person listening often becomes angry as well. After you have worked through your anger, that other person may remain angry and be unable to forgive. Jesus' plan is that we go directly to the person with whom we are angry.

If you are afraid that your anger may explode, get alone with God before confronting the person and tell Him all the hurts and anger you are feeling. You may also need to write down the angry emotions you are experiencing to release some of the tension. After this, pray earnestly, asking God to give you His love for that person and His direction as you go to that person. Also ask Him to reveal any areas in which you are to blame for the situation. If there are any areas for which you are to blame, ask that person's forgiveness before you express your feelings of anger. Then after expressing those feelings, be ready to forgive.

Read Matthew 18:21-22. What did Jesus teach about forgiveness?

_____

_____

_____

What needs to be done after we have put the past behind us (see Philippians 3:13-14)?

_____

_____

_____

Why is it important to reach forward?

_____

_____

_____

What are some ways that this could be accomplished?

_____
_____
_____
_____

Read 1 Peter 2:2. What are we to desire?

_____
_____
_____
_____

What will be the result?

_____
_____
_____
_____

Read 2 Peter 1:5-11 in several different Bible translations. What qualities are Christians encouraged to cultivate?

_____
_____
_____
_____

What effort should be put into cultivating these qualities (see verses 5,8)?

_____
_____
_____
_____

What words in verse 8 indicate a growing relationship with God?

_____
_____
_____
_____

Why do you think it is important to have those qualities in increasing amounts?

_____

_____

_____

_____

In verse 10, what does Peter ask us to do?

_____

_____

_____

_____

What does God promise to a person who is growing and practicing his or her Christianity (see verses 10-11)?

_____

_____

_____

A Closer Look at My Own Heart

According to 2 Peter 1:10, every Christian should examine his or her life to make certain that he or she belongs to God. What is God saying to you? Are you certain that you belong to God?

_____

_____

_____

One characteristic of a true child of God is a desire to grow and become fruitful in God's kingdom. When we are in a growing and fruitful relationship with God, we will not be constantly stumbling. In contrast, the Christian who is not growing is usually going backwards and is open to numerous attacks from Satan. An immature Christian stumbles often and is probably one of the most discontented of God's creations. Read 2 Corinthians 4:16. What does Paul say about a Christian's inner self?

_____

_____

_____

How do you think Paul's inner self was being renewed?

_____

_____

_____

_____

Do you think it is important that a Christian's inner self be renewed daily? Why or why not?

_____

_____

_____

_____

Read Philippians 1:6. What is God seeking to do in your life?

_____

_____

_____

_____

How long will this process go on?

_____

_____

_____

_____

God's desire is to perfect (complete) each one of us. What are some ways in which you restrict God's work to perfect your life?

_____

_____

_____

_____

How does this affect your joy and contentment?

_____

_____

_____

_____

What do you need to do to allow God to do His work of perfecting in your life?

_____

_____

_____

_____

_____

Paul would never have found contentment in Christ had he not been a growing Christian. The same is true today. The Christian who is not growing is not content. If our desire is to press forward in Christ to our highest potential, it is essential that we spend time with God and His Word. The Scriptures are our spiritual food; and without them we will be weak, ineffective and discontented Christians.

Just as we need the Scriptures, we also need the help and encouragement of other believers. We are not strong enough to fight Satan's attacks alone. We need the strength of God's Word and the support of God's people (see Hebrews 10:24-25).

Sometimes Christians feel that they are strong enough in the Lord and don't need the support of other Christians. This is one of Satan's deceptions. God commands us to stimulate one another to love and good works and to encourage each other. We cannot do this if we are not getting together. We cannot help to carry each other's burdens (see Galatians 6:2). We need other believers to help us grow in the Lord.

Action Steps I Can Take Today

Read through the following questions, and then choose the action step that most closely matches your present spiritual need.

If you have a problem with guilt because of past sins, read Romans 8:1 and Colossians 1:21-22. What do these verses say about those who are in Christ Jesus?

_____

_____

_____

_____

How do these verses make you feel about yourself?

_____

_____

_____

_____

Appropriate one of the verses for yourself by either memorizing or paraphrasing it in your own words and writing it down on a small index card. Carry the card with you as a reminder of the truth written on it.

Is there someone you need to ask to forgive you? If there is, go to God in prayer. Ask Him to give you wisdom, insight and courage. Also ask a Christian friend to pray with you and for you. Ask him or her to keep you accountable to do what you know God is calling you to do.

Is there anger in your life that you need to deal with? Reread the section "Dealing with Unresolved Anger." Prayerfully consider how God wants you to deal with your specific anger. Then ask a Christian friend to be your prayer partner as you act upon what God reveals to you.

Do you want to grow in the Lord? If so, determine to make it a practice to meet with other believers regularly and to spend time daily in God's Word. Ask God to give you a partner who will encourage you in these areas on a regular basis—someone you can also encourage in the same way.

SEVEN

OBEY GOD

When God spoke to him, Paul immediately obeyed. One of the reasons he was able to do so was that he had his eyes on eternal benefits. He sought to lay up treasures in heaven rather than treasures on earth. In this chapter, we will discuss the importance of obeying God, and we will also see how seeking eternal rewards rather than earthly possessions will help us find peace and contentment, even in difficult circumstances.

A Closer Look at the Problem

It isn't always easy to obey God, but it is even harder on us when we choose not to obey Him. Disobedience always carries a price tag, and the price is always high. Briefly describe an experience in your life when disobedience kept you from peace with God.

_____

_____

_____

_____

Now describe an experience in which obedience brought you peace with God.

_____

_____

_____

_____

Disobedience robs many Christians of peace and contentment. If there is some area of willful disobedience in our lives, we cannot experience total peace with God. When we knowingly continue to commit sin, it creates a barrier between us and God (and ultimately results in punishment if we don't repent). We hesitate to come into His presence because we know the sin is there, and guilt robs us of our joy in the Lord.

Guilt over past sins and failures was one of the roadblocks we examined in the previous chapter, but if we continue to sin, we will continue to experience guilt. That guilt will keep us from finding joy and peace with God. We must repent of that sin in order to find peace. This means that we, through God's power within us, stop sinning and turn our eyes on Jesus. It means that we develop a lifestyle of obedience to Jesus Christ.

A Closer Look at God's Truth

One of the most important things we can learn from the apostle Paul is obedience. His focus was on Jesus and because it was, he could exhort the Philippians to watch him and do the things he did.

Read Acts 16:9-10. What direction did Paul receive from God in these verses?

_____

_____

_____

_____

How long did it take him to obey?

_____

_____

_____

Reread Acts 26:16-19. What was Paul's response to this vision from God (see verse 19)?

_____

_____

_____

What do these Scriptures from Acts tell you about Paul's relationship with God?

_____

_____

_____

_____

Read Philippians 3:12-18. What attitude did Paul encourage in those who want to mature in the Lord (see verses 13-14)?

_____

_____

_____

_____

How would that attitude help a person toward perfection, or maturity?

_____

_____

_____

_____

What was the first thing Paul encouraged the Philippians to do?

_____

_____

_____

What two other actions were the Philippians encouraged to do (see verse 17)?

_____

_____

_____

What warning did Paul give in verse 18?

_____

_____

_____

How does what Paul wrote in verses 17 and 18 apply to us today?

_____

_____

_____

What responsibilities do we have to those who may be watching us and following our example?

_____

_____

_____

Read Philippians 2:12-16. What role does obedience play in working out our salvation (see verses 15-16)?

_____

_____

_____

_____

What did Paul say the Philippians had done before (see verse 12)?

_____

_____

_____

_____

What did he encourage them to continue doing (see verses 12,14,16)?

_____

_____

_____

When Paul spoke of working out our salvation, he did not mean that we are saved by our own works (see verse 12). He meant that we are responsible for cooperating in the process of our own sanctification. Sanctification is the process by which we become more like Christ and in which our salvation is perfected. By our free will, we unite ourselves to Christ, agree to be transformed by God's grace, and experience His eternal presence. But ultimately it is God who works in us to make us holy and to set us apart for His purposes according to His will (see Philippians 2:13).

God has invited us to be saved and to be made holy. It is up to us to believe in Jesus and accept what He has done for us (see John 6:27-29). Once we have received Christ, we have a responsibility to work toward spiritual growth in Christ, accepting Him as master of our lives and allowing Him to take control. Unless we are willing to obey, we will not grow in Him and we will not experience His peace and contentment.

What is God's part in our growth and obedience (see verses 13-16)?

_____

_____

_____

_____

According to verse 14, what should our attitude be as we obey?

_____

_____

_____

_____

What are the results of cheerful obedience?

_____

_____

_____

_____

What part does obedience play in proving ourselves "blameless and innocent" (verse 14)?

_____

_____

_____

How does our obedience affect other people?

_____

_____

_____

Read 1 Peter 3:1-2. What result of obedience is found in these verses?

_____

_____

_____

If we want to be able to reach other people for God, our obedience to Him is essential. We cannot continue to live in sin and be a light to the world. People will see the way we act, and our sinful actions will negate our words. We will also be reluctant to share because we will feel defeated, and our peace and contentment will have disappeared. Reread Philippians 1:27-28. What did Paul urge?

_____

_____

_____

_____

How would you describe a life that is lived "in a manner worthy of the gospel of Christ" (verse 27)?

_____

_____

_____

_____

What will be the results of such a lifestyle?

_____

_____

_____

_____

How does obedience help us to stand firm in the Lord?

_____

_____

_____

_____

How does obedience unite believers?

_____

_____

_____

_____

When Christ died on the cross, He conquered Satan and freed us from Satan's power. A believer does not have to be a slave to sin. We have a choice. Paul was asking the Philippians to choose to live a life of victory over sin rather than a life of surrender to sin. Read Romans 6:1-18. List all verses that tell us we are not to continue to sin.

_____

_____

_____

How should we live, according to verse 4?

_____

_____

_____

How did Jesus make this possible?

_____
_____
_____
_____

How are we to think of ourselves (see verse 11)?

_____
_____
_____

What happens when we believe that God's power is greater than the power of sin (see verse 18)?

_____
_____
_____

List all verses that imply we have a choice of whether we serve Christ or sin.

_____
_____
_____

What is the result of our choice (see verse 19)?

_____
_____
_____

List all verses that indicate we are not powerless to allow sin to control us.

_____
_____
_____

One reason many of us Christians live defeated and unhappy lives is because we do not claim the power of God to overcome sin. We try to obey in our strength and we fail. We try again and we fail again. After a while we quit trying because we feel that it is useless to fight. God, however, has promised that there is no temptation that is beyond our ability to overcome it; He is faithful to provide a way of escape (see 1 Corinthians 10:13).

Our responsibility is to choose to ask God for His help and to take the way of escape that He provides. If every time we face a temptation we stop and ask God for His power that overcame sin at the cross, He will provide an escape for us. Sometimes we, as Christians, do not want God's way in our lives, and we do not ask for His help. As a result, we continue to fall victim to sin's power and are miserable, discontented people.

Read John 14:21. When you obey Jesus, what sort of relationship will you have with God?

_____

_____

_____

Read James 1:22-27. How is the person who hears the Word but does not act upon it described (see verses 23-24)?

_____

_____

_____

How is the person who hears God's Word and responds with obedience described (see verse 25)?

_____

_____

_____

What is pure religion (see verse 27)?

_____

_____

_____

We see from these verses that pure religion in the sight of God is a religion that produces action. We can study God's Word all day and be with God's people often; but unless we are willing to obey God, our religion is empty and we are deluding ourselves. Read Philippians 3:18-21. What had caused Paul to weep (see verse 18)?

_____

_____

_____

How did Paul describe them (see verse 19)?

_____
_____
_____
_____

What effect does our goal in life have upon our obedience to God?

_____
_____
_____
_____

How can Christians become enemies of the cross?

_____
_____
_____

According to verses 20-21, what was Paul's focus in life?

_____
_____
_____

How did Paul's focus affect his style of living (see verse 17)?

_____
_____
_____

If we want to obey God, we need to seek God's promise of eternal life (our spiritual reward) rather than strive for earthly possessions and benefits (rewards of the flesh). The people described by Paul as enemies of the cross had sought earthly rewards and as a result their lives failed to honor God and had actually damaged the cause of Christ. In contrast, Paul's focus on an eternal goal led to an exemplary life others could follow.

Read Colossians 3:1-2. What did Paul urge the Colossians to seek?

_____
_____
_____

What was Paul's focus of attention in the following verses?

Romans 8:18

_____

_____

_____

2 Corinthians 4:16–5:10

_____

_____

_____

Philippians 1:21-23

_____

_____

_____

Philippians 3:11

_____

_____

_____

Philippians 3:14

_____

_____

_____

How did Paul's focus and goal help him to obey God?

_____

_____

_____

What effect did Paul's focus and goal have on his joy and contentment?

_____

_____

_____

Think back to the last time you willingly chose to disobey God. What was your focus at that time?

_____

_____

_____

_____

What happened to your joy and contentment?

_____

_____

_____

_____

Many people are putting all their energies into seeking and caring for earthly treasures. We work so hard for material possessions that we neglect to lay up treasures in heaven. We don't have the time or energy to work on a right relationship with God or get involved with helping others to know the Lord. We don't have the time and energy to train our children in the Lord or to teach them to pray. We don't have enough money left to give to the Lord; we're too busy paying for and caring for our material possessions. Yet material possessions can never bring lasting joy or contentment (see Matthew 16:26).

A Closer Look at My Own Heart

One reason Paul found contentment was because he obeyed God and sought heavenly treasures. Things of this earth were not important to him. Being in prison could not take him away from his goal. Being hungry did not change his focus. In the same way, if we desire God's contentment, we must get our focus and our desire off earthly things and onto spiritual goals.

Jesus emphasized the difference between the earthly and the spiritual when He gave His Sermon on the Mount. Read Matthew 6:19-21. How can you lay up "treasures in heaven" (verse 20)?

_____

_____

_____

_____

What part does obedience play in laying up treasures in heaven?

_____
_____
_____
_____
_____

How do you think laying up treasures in heaven will affect your joy and contentment?

_____
_____
_____
_____
_____

Action Steps I Can Take Today

Write down a spiritual goal that you would like to make your focus this year. Share your goal with a Christian friend who will help keep you accountable. You might even want to get together and brainstorm practical ideas you can put into action to help you attain your goal.

_____
_____
_____
_____
_____

In Philippians 4:13, Paul states, "I can do all things through Him [Christ] who strengthens me." Rewrite this verse in your own words to claim victory over a sin you want to overcome. Every time you are tempted, claim that victory and ask God for His power to overcome. He will not fail you.

_____
_____
_____
_____

$\mathscr{S}$ET PROPER PRIORITIES AND DEVELOP YOUR MINISTRY

In the last chapter, we learned how important obeying God is in order for us to be content. We also learned that when we keep our focus on Jesus Christ and when we seek heavenly treasures rather than earthly ones, we can find contentment in any circumstance.

In this chapter, we will learn about setting priorities that please God and that result in the joy that comes from giving and receiving love. We will also learn the importance of every Christian having a ministry, and we will briefly examine some of the different types of ministry that are important to the Body of Christ today. Particular emphasis in this final chapter on finding contentment will be on the ministries of encouragement, giving, peacemaking and prayer.

PART ONE: SET PROPER PRIORITIES

Because Paul was seeking eternal goals, he had the right priorities in his life. In order for us to have contentment in Christ, we also need to get our priorities straight. As we make pleasing God our number one priority, we will naturally reach out to others with the love and unselfishness of Christ.

A Closer Look at the Problem

An important characteristic in Paul's life that led to his contentment was following Jesus' example of humility and unselfishness. Paul did not seek to advance his own cause. Instead, he willingly gave of himself so that others could benefit. Because he acted that way, he was not susceptible to the depression that can come when personal desires are denied.

Often, we try to grasp what we think will make us happy. We try to hang on to our rights, our needs, our desires, and we end up being miserable. Jesus willingly gave up His position of equality with God to meet our needs. As a result, God has exalted His name above all names and given Him great honor.

When we give up our rights and our desires and put the needs of others first, we will find a joy and contentment that can never come from grasping what we think will make us happy. When we put others first, God will exalt us and give us His peace and contentment.

A Closer Look at God's Truth

Read 2 Corinthians 5:9. What was Paul's goal?

_____

_____

_____

_____

How do you think Paul's goal affected his relationship with other people?

_____

_____

_____

_____

How do you think Paul's goal affected his peace and contentment?

_____

_____

_____

_____

Paul's goal was to honor Christ and be pleasing to Him. He wanted to live in such a way that he would never bring shame to Christ. Because honoring Christ was his goal, *circumstances* could not stop him from achieving what he sought. Being in prison, being hungry or cold, other people and their opinions—nothing could keep him from honoring Christ and pleasing Him. That choice rested in *his* control. In the same way, we choose where we set our priorities. If our top priority is to please God, no outside influence can keep us from our goal.

Read Philippians 2:1-11. Compare Jesus' goal in life to Paul's goal. How are they similar?

_____

_____

_____

What was necessary in Jesus' life for Him to accomplish His goal (see verses 6-8)?

_____

_____

_____

List all the phrases in verses 5-8 that show who Jesus was and what He became for us.

_____

_____

_____

How does verse 4 relate to what Jesus became?

_____

_____

_____

What did Jesus do when He became a man (see verse 7)?

_____

_____

_____

What could Jesus have held on to instead (see verse 6)?

_____

_____

_____

How do you think Jesus "emptied Himself" (verse 7), or "made himself nothing" (*NIV*)?

_____

_____

_____

What indication do we have that Jesus had a choice in this matter?

_____

_____

_____

Choosing humility and unselfishness goes against our human nature. We want to feel important and have all our needs met, but Jesus did just the opposite. He gave up both His human and His divine rights. How did Paul define "unselfishness" (see verse 4)?

_____

_____

_____

How did Paul define "humility" (see verse 3)?

_____

_____

_____

What was the result of Jesus' unselfishness and humility for us?

_____

_____

_____

What was the result of Jesus' unselfishness and humility for Him (see verses 9-11)?

_____

_____

_____

How does unselfishness affect our learning to be content?

_____

_____

_____

What effect does humility have on our being content?

_____

_____

_____

How would following Jesus' example of humility and unselfishness change your life? How would following Jesus make a difference in the lives of those around you?

_____

_____

_____

_____

Paul knew that Christians living together in harmony had power to impact the world. Therefore, he encouraged the Philippians to be of one mind and one heart. What would a united church show (see verse 1)?

_____

_____

_____

_____

How do Paul's instructions in verses 3 and 4 relate to a united church?

_____

_____

_____

Read Philippians 4:1-5. What phrases show that Paul loved the Philippians?

_____

_____

_____

_____

What instruction did Paul give to the Philippians (see verse 1)?

_____

_____

_____

_____

What did Paul urge Euodia and Syntyche to do (see verse 2)?

_____

_____

_____

_____

What did he urge the rest of the Philippians to do for Euodia and Syntyche (see verse 3)?

_____

_____

_____

What had these women done in the past (see verse 3)?

_____

_____

_____

What did Paul encourage all the Philippians to do (see verse 5)?

_____

_____

_____

How would the instructions in verse 5 help the Philippians live in harmony?

_____

_____

_____

The Body of Christ is in danger when even two members are not living in harmony. A divided church may begin with just two people disagreeing; before long, there is a division throughout the congregation. Paul urged the two Philippian women to have a gentle, harmonious spirit that would allow them to be reconciled and continue loving each other even after being hurt.

A divided church cannot move forward. The lack of contentment will be obvious to all the believers, and they will find worship difficult because there is a tension that makes it hard to feel the presence of God. Contentment and joy disappear. Unbelievers who see the division and tension will associate Christ with the bickering and lack of love they see. This will give them a reason to want no part of the church or its Savior.

Read Philippians 1:7-11. How did Paul express his love for the Philippians in these verses?

_____

_____

_____

What do you think Paul meant by "the affection of Christ Jesus" (verse 8)?

_____

_____

_____

How is Christ's love different from natural love?

_____

_____

_____

What was Paul's prayer for the Philippians (see verse 9)?

_____

_____

_____

Why does love need to have knowledge and discernment (see verses 10-11)?

_____

_____

_____

_____

Is it possible to love someone in a way that is not beneficial for that person? Give an example of such a person.

_____

_____

_____

What results in the Christian's life come from love with knowledge and discernment?

_____

_____

_____

How can love with knowledge and discernment help us "approve the things that are excellent" (verse 10)?

_____

_____

_____

What will be the result for God?

_____

_____

_____

Who is the source of our fruitfulness (see verse 11)?

_____

_____

_____

_____

Paul loved the Philippians. As they had worked together and shared both joys and sorrows, he had come to care about them deeply. In the same way, when we share our hurts, our joys and our ministries, we will grow to deeply love those who become our partners.

Paul also expressed a need for the Philippian believers to have the right kind of love. They needed to embody Jesus' love, which showed itself in a servant's attitude and humility. That is exactly what we need to embody as well.

We need to be careful, however, about how we love. Sometimes our love can be grasping, smothering, overprotective or overpermissive. We need to pray for God's knowledge and discernment so that our love will be beneficial to us, to the person we love and to the kingdom of God.

Read John 15:9-13. What did Jesus promise to His followers (see verse 10)?

_____

_____

_____

What was the condition of the promise?

_____

_____

_____

Why did Jesus say these things to them (see verse 11)?

_____

_____

_____

What commandment did Jesus give to them (see verse 12)?

_____

_____

_____

_____

How does the commandment in verse 12 relate to the promises in verses 10 and 11?

_____

_____

_____

_____

What part does loving others play in our experiencing joy?

_____

_____

_____

What did Jesus do to prove His great love for us (see verse 13)?

_____

_____

_____

How does a person love as Jesus loved?

_____

_____

_____

What difference would it make in the lives of those around us if we loved with Jesus' kind of love?

_____

_____

_____

How do verses 12 and 13 relate to Paul's words in Philippians 2:3-4?

_____

_____

_____

Read John 15:14-17. What are the results of obeying Jesus' commands?

_____

_____

_____

_____

What command did Jesus reemphasize in verse 17?

_____

_____

_____

_____

As Jesus taught His disciples to love one another, He gave them keys to open the doors of joy and contentment (see John 15:11). One of the keys, given in John 15:14-17, is obedience.

The disciples could not experience the close relationship of a friend without being obedient. As Jesus gave them the condition of obedience, He also gave them the commandment to love each other. As they obeyed, they would experience a special closeness to God and to fellow believers. They would produce a fruitful harvest and their prayers would be answered. Joy and contentment would result.

Jesus taught His disciples to love in the same way that He had loved them—with an unselfish love that puts the interests of others above the interests of self. One of our most basic needs in life is to be loved and to have others express love for us. As we reach out with Christ's love, that need will be met. We will experience the joy that comes from being loved.

Read John 17:20-23. List all the phrases from these verses that indicate Jesus' desire for His disciples to be united in love.

_____

_____

_____

If all believers were united in love, what would be the result for the world (see verses 21,23)?

_____

_____

_____

What part does the giving and accepting of love play in the perfecting of Christians?

_____

_____

_____

Summarize in your own words why loving God and others is so important.

_____

_____

_____

A Closer Look at My Own Heart

As Jesus poured out His heart in prayer to His Father, He again stressed the urgency of our loving one another. When we Christians genuinely love each other, unbelievers notice the difference in our lives and in our relationships. If Christians loved as Christ intended, nothing could keep the world away. Genuine Christlike love makes the unbeliever want what the Christian has. When we Christians genuinely love each other, we also benefit tremendously. We look out for each other. We help each other and, as a result, we encourage each other to the highest level of spiritual maturity possible.

Read Hebrews 10:24-25. What are we commanded to do?

_____

_____

_____

What are some ways that other believers have stimulated your love toward others?

_____

_____

_____

What can you do that will stimulate love in others? List a few practical and specific actions.

_____

_____

_____

Read 1 Corinthians 13:4-7. How is love described in this familiar passage?

_____

_____

_____

_____

There are times when it may be humanly impossible for us to love a person who has hurt us or those whom we care about. During those times, we need to be honest with God and tell Him exactly how we feel. Then we need to ask God to fill us with *His* love for that person.

It is important not to confuse feelings of love with actions of love (described in 1 Corinthians 13:4-7 and 1 John 3:17-18). God commands us to act in love. As we obey His commands, the feelings of love will follow. As we stimulate others to love, God's love will grow within our own hearts.

Action Steps I Can Take Today

Is there someone you have difficulty loving? Memorize 1 Corinthians 13:4-7 and ask God to give you this kind of love. Paraphrasing these truths into a prayer for that person will further transform your emotions and your actions. You will experience God's love in its fullness.

Review the things Paul wanted to accomplish with his life by rereading Philippians 1:20-21 in several different Bible translations, and then write in your own words what Paul was saying. How do his priorities compare with yours?

_____

_____

_____

_____

How will your tomorrows be different because of the priorities you're choosing today?

_____

_____

_____

_____

_____

PART TWO: DEVELOP YOUR MINISTRY

In part one, we saw that Paul set proper priorities for himself and that Paul's first priority was to be pleasing to Christ. He wanted to honor and exalt Jesus in everything he did and, because of this, his actions toward people were pleasing to God. He was able to reach out to others in humility with Christlike love. As he freely gave love, he received the joy of being loved in return.

One of the results of Paul's loving others was a desire to minister to them. As he served others, he experienced a sense of worth and accomplishment that enhanced his contentment in all circumstances.

A Closer Look at the Problem

Paul wanted to be with the Lord, but his love for the Philippians and his desire to help them grow overpowered his longing. He knew that he was needed on earth and that his ministry would accomplish results. He was not afraid of work, nor did he expect others to serve him. His expectation and desire for life was fruitful labor.

Some people today look at the Church as something to serve them and to meet their needs. However, one of our basic needs is to be needed and to be useful to others. This need can only be met as we are willing to serve others and become their ministers. Contrary to popular opinion, leisure time does not bring joy and contentment. Fruitful labor does.

A Closer Look at God's Truth

Reread Philippians 1:12-18. What evidence of Paul's ministry, even though he was in prison, do you see in these verses?

_____

_____

_____

_____

What motives for ministry did Paul list (see verses 15-17)?

_____

_____

_____

_____

Which motives are noble ones (see verses 15-16)?

_____

_____

_____

Read Romans 1:15-17. What was Paul's desire?

_____

_____

_____

Why did he desire to minister in this way?

_____

_____

_____

What do verses 16 and 17 indicate about the power of the gospel?

_____

_____

_____

How do these verses in Romans relate to Paul's ability to rejoice even though people were preaching from wrong motives (see Philippians 1:18)?

_____

_____

_____

What do the verses in Romans reveal about Paul's ministry and his feelings about that ministry?

_____

_____

_____

We can see from these verses that Paul had a ministry of preaching the gospel of Jesus Christ. He could rejoice when others preached, even from wrong motives, because he knew the important point was that the gospel *was being* preached and the truth was being made known. Paul knew that as people heard the gospel, their lives would change and they would be drawn to the Lord in a faith relationship.

THE MINISTRY OF ENCOURAGEMENT
Reread Philippians 1:21-26. What two desires did Paul express?

_____

_____

_____

_____

What reasons did he give for wanting to remain alive (see verses 24-26)?

_____

_____

_____

_____

What do these verses reveal about Paul's love and unselfishness?

_____

_____

_____

Why are these virtues important if we want to minister to others?

_____

_____

_____

_____

Read Philippians 2:19-24. How did Paul describe Timothy?

_____

_____

_____

How did Timothy differ from the other people (see verse 20-21)?

_____

_____

_____

How had Timothy proved his worth (see verse 22)?

_____

_____

_____

What phrase describes Timothy's humility (see verse 22)?

_____

_____

_____

Why is it important that people minister with the right motives?

_____

_____

_____

Why are proper motives important in finding contentment and peace?

_____

_____

_____

_____

Most of us desire a ministry—we want to be useful. But often, our motives are not pure. We each want a job that will bring recognition and honor, and we tend to shy away from those jobs that bring no glory or no notice at all. We would rather be an officer than be on the cleanup committee or on nursery duty. In contrast, Timothy served with Paul like a humble child serving his father. He was willing to take the lowly position of a servant, and because he had a servant attitude, God was able to use him and gave him an effective ministry. Read Philippians 2:25-30. How is Epaphroditus described?

_____

_____

_____

What words prove that Epaphroditus loved the Philippians (see verse 26)?

_____

_____

_____

What emotion did Paul expect the Philippians to experience at Epaphroditus's return to them (see verse 28)?

_____

_____

_____

How did Paul instruct them to receive Epaphroditus (see verses 29-30)? Why?

_____

_____

_____

How did Paul look upon Epaphroditus's healing (see verse 27)? Why?

_____

_____

_____

Why do you think Paul felt the way he did about Epaphroditus's having been near death?

_____

_____

_____

Why did Paul not feel the same way about his own death?

_____

_____

_____

_____

Paul had a deep love for Epaphroditus. In spite of his strong belief in a better hereafter with Jesus, Paul knew that he would miss Epaphroditus if he died. In the same way, we need to acknowledge that Christians go through difficult times and that it is normal to feel sad when we have experienced a loss or a deep hurt. God can and will give us peace in the midst of those trials and will use them to strengthen us and enlarge our ministry to others. Our ministry to others may also include encouraging and strengthening those who serve the Lord, just as Paul instructed the Philippians to do to Epaphroditus and others like him (see verse 28).

Reread Philippians 4:10-19. In what way had the Philippians ministered to Paul?

_____

_____

_____

In what way was Paul ministering to them?

_____

_____

_____

_____

What was the result of the Philippians' ministry in Paul's life?

_____

_____

_____

_____

How do you think the Philippians' ministry to Paul made them feel?

_____

_____

_____

_____

How does verse 19 relate to joy and contentment?

_____

_____

_____

THE MINISTRY OF GIVING
Read 2 Corinthians 9:6-15. What does verse 6 tell us about our giving?

_____

_____

_____

What are some of the things that God may want us to give cheerfully?

_____

_____

_____

What does God promise in verse 8?

_____

_____

_____

List the promises found in verses 10 and 11, and give a spiritual application for each of them.

Promise	Application

How are these promises related to the cheerful giving of ourselves?

_____

_____

_____

Giving liberally and cheerfully of ourselves and our resources results in an abundance for God, an abundance for the giver, and an abundance for others. The promises of these verses are an example of the way God will bless us when we cheerfully give of ourselves to His kingdom and to the service of others. These promises apply any time we willingly give of ourselves and our resources in ministry to Christ.

THE MINISTRY OF PEACEMAKING
Reread Philippians 4:2-3. What ministry did Paul urge?

_____

_____

_____

What did Paul say these women had done in the past?

_____

_____

_____

What term did Paul use to describe those who had ministered with him?

_____

_____

_____

What did Paul say about those who had worked with him?

_____

_____

_____

In these verses, Paul advocated a ministry that perhaps few people think of as a ministry: He urged the Philippians to be peacemakers. Jesus came to make peace with God and with others possible. In the same way, God wants us to work toward bringing others to peace with Him and with one another. He even promised a special blessing to peacemakers (see Matthew 5:9). Read 2 Corinthians 5:18-21. What ministry did Paul have (see verse 18)?

_____

_____

_____

What ministry did Jesus have (see verse 19)?

_____

_____

_____

What effect should Jesus' ministry have in your life (see verses 20-21)?

_____

_____

_____

There are people all around us who need help in finding peace with God and peace with others. This ministry needs to be encouraged in every child of God. You can be part of it by asking God to bring to your awareness people whom you can help with a ministry of reconciliation. Become involved with those people, and let God's truth and light shine through you.

THE MINISTRY OF PRAYER
Read Ephesians 6:18-20. Who did Paul encourage the Ephesians to minister to in prayer? How often did he want them to practice this ministry?

_____

_____

_____

Prayer is probably one of the most important of all ministries. Jesus often arose while it was still dark to go and pray. Before He chose the 12 apostles, He spent the entire night in prayer. At Gethsemane He spent hours in prayer, gaining strength to face the cross. Likewise, any effective ministry we are going to have must begin with prayer. Often, praying for people is more effective than preaching to them. There are some ministries that are open to only a few. Prayer is open to all.

SPIRITUAL GIFTS

Understanding our spiritual giftedness will also help us develop our ministries. Read 1 Corinthians 12. What did Paul tell the Corinthians about spiritual gifts in verses 4 through 7?

_____

_____

_____

_____

List the gifts and the ministries described in verses 8-11,28.

_____

_____

_____

How does the example of a body illustrate the truths Paul was teaching about spiritual gifts?

_____

_____

_____

How do verses 11-27 relate to the different gifts and ministries described in this chapter?

_____

_____

_____

What truth did Paul discuss in verses 22-24?

_____

_____

_____

What will be the result of accepting this truth (see verses 25-26)?

_____

_____

_____

What point was Paul making in verses 29 and 30?

_____

_____

_____

Paul was stressing that not all Christians are going to have the same gifts or the same ministries. God created us to be different and has given to each of us special gifts for different ministries. We should never feel that we are more spiritual than the person whose gift is different from ours.

Although God planned us to be different, He also planned for us to work together as the parts of a body do. People who we may feel are insignificant are tremendously important in God's plan. Sometimes a person's gifts and ministries are unseen by others, but they are seen by God and are essential for the functioning of His Body as a whole.

A Closer Look at My Own Heart

Read 2 Timothy 3:14-17. What will help prepare you for ministry?

_____

_____

_____

According to these verses, what will the Scriptures do for you?

_____

_____

_____

What part will the study of Scripture have in you becoming a more effective minister for Jesus Christ?

_____

_____

_____

Often, we Christians want an immediate and glamorous ministry. We get frustrated at the Church for not realizing our potential and providing us with our desired place of ministry. We need to realize that we must develop a personal relationship with Jesus before He can give us a ministry. Sometimes He even has a better ministry for us than the one we think we want. If we take the time to develop our relationship with Christ, a ministry will naturally follow. This ministry will be a productive one for the Body of Christ and a source of satisfaction and contentment for us.

Look back over this lesson, and then complete the following sentences:

Paul's purpose in life was . . .

_____
_____
_____
_____

Timothy's purpose in life was . . .

_____
_____
_____
_____

Epaphroditus's purpose in life was . . .

_____
_____
_____

According to Matthew 20:25-28, Jesus' purpose in life was . . .

_____
_____
_____

My purpose in life is . . .

_____
_____
_____

Action Steps I Can Take Today

Carefully examine the spiritual gifts listed in 1 Corinthians 12, and ask God to help you see which gift you have. Then determine to develop your relationship with God so that you can effectively use your gift in ministry to others. What specific steps will you take to develop your relationship with God (spend time daily with Him in prayer, participate in a Bible study, and so forth)?

_____

_____

_____

_____

What specific steps will you take to use your spiritual gift this week?

_____

_____

_____

_____

Always remember that God loves a cheerful and generous giver, and one of the things you can give is your time.

Finally, as you complete this Bible study, remember this: Jesus Christ came that you might have life abundantly. His desire for you is that you experience peace, joy and contentment, not just now in the present, but also throughout eternity.

Post the following verse where you can see it: "For to me, to live is Christ and to die is gain" (Philippians 1:21). As you walk through your day, rejoice. As you serve God, sing. He loves you and will work all things together for your good.

Lord, I want to be used by You. I ask that You develop within me a close relationship to You that will overflow to bless the lives of others. Give me the desire and the willingness to spend the time necessary to develop that relationship. Establish within me a servant's heart that will give cheerfully of myself and my resources to You and to others. Thank You for the ministry You are developing in me right now.

FINDING CONTENTMENT LEADER'S GUIDE

The purpose of this leader's guide is to provide those willing to lead a group Bible study with additional material to make the study more effective. Each lesson has one or two exercises designed to increase participation and lead the group members into closer relationship with their heavenly Father.

The exercises are designed to introduce the study and emphasize the theme of the chapter. When two exercises are suggested, it is up to your discretion whether to use them both. Time will probably be the deciding factor.

If the group is larger than six members, you may want to break into smaller groups for the personal sharing time so that all will have an adequate opportunity to share. As the lessons proceed, the exercises will invite more personal sharing. Keep these two important points in mind:

1. Involve each member of the group in the discussion when possible. Some may be too shy or new to the Bible study experience. Be sensitive to their needs and encourage them to answer simple questions that do not require personal information or biblical knowledge. As they get more comfortable in the group, they will probably share more often.

2. Make a commitment with the group members that what is shared in the discussion times and prayer requests must be kept in strictest confidence.

After each lesson, be prepared to pray with those who have special needs or concerns. Emphasize the truth of God's Word as you minister to the group members, leading them to a closer relationship with their Lord and Savior.

ONE

TRUST IN JESUS

Objective

To help group members understand that Jesus is trustworthy and that we must choose to put our complete trust in Him.

Preparation

EXERCISE 1

Prepare two identical sets of placards by writing each of one of the following professions on a separate 6" x 12" sheet of posterboard or construction paper: nurses, teachers, military officers, clergy, police officers, bankers, auto mechanics, journalists, lawyers, business executives, congressmen, advertisers and lobbyists. Place the two stacks of cards in two separate piles and mix up the order of each set.

EXERCISE 2

Find out if anyone in your group or church family regularly does journaling as a part of his or her spiritual journey. Invite that person to share with the group how and why they do it and what experiences he or she has had in the process. Or prepare to share your own experiences. To encourage journaling for your group members, obtain some inexpensive notebooks to give to group members as they leave this week's session.

DISCUSSION

Familiarize yourself with the questions in the following "Group Participation" section, and choose which questions you definitely want to discuss with the group. Note that there might not be time to discuss every question, so modify or adapt this discussion guide to fit the needs of your group. Additional discussion questions/action steps are provided to stimulate further discussion if you have the time.

Group Participation

EXERCISE 1

Divide the group in half and give one set of cards to each group. Play a game of "Who Do We Trust?" by giving the groups two minutes to arrange the cards in the order of the public's trust in the listed professions. After two minutes, have each group share their order, with the number one, most-trusted profession first to the least-trusted profession last. After both groups have shared, read off the following order:

1. Nurses
2. Teachers
3. Military officers
4. Clergy
5. Police officers
6. Bankers
7. Auto mechanics
8. Journalists
9. Lawyers
10. Business executives
11. Congressmen
12. Advertisers
13. Lobbyists*

* "Public Ranks Nurses, Pharmacists and Doctors as Trustworthy Professionals," BioTechnology, December 4, 2008. http://bloggingbiotech.wordpress.com/2008/12/04/public-ranks-nurses-pharmacists-docs-as-trustworthy-professionals.

Take a few minutes to discuss why they think people perceive certain professionals to be more trusted than others. Relate our trust in other people to how we can always trust the Lord.

EXERCISE 2

Have the volunteer and/or you share about the practice of journaling. Invite group members to ask questions about the process. Give each member one of the notebooks you obtained and encourage them to try it for the remainder of this study. If you are new to journaling, be honest with the group members about that fact and invite them to start this journey with you.

DISCUSSION

1. Discuss the following questions (or the ones you have chosen) from the "A Closer Look at God's Truth" section:

   • How did Paul demonstrate his faith in Christ according to the incidents recorded in Acts 16:6-40? What are the various ways that his faith was tested as recorded in this passage?

- What are some of the ways the Holy Spirit directs people today? Invite a volunteer or two to briefly share a specific time that they were led by the Holy Spirit.

- Read 1 John 4:4. What are some ways Satan attacks Christians today? What is the promise given in 1 John 4:4?

- Read James 4:7. What are some subtle ways that Satan tries to tempt us? What are some ways that Christians can "resist the devil" so that he will flee from them?

- What are some of the gods or idols people worship today instead of the one true God?

2. Discuss the following questions (or the ones you have chosen) from the "A Closer Look at My Own Heart" section:

- What are some of the gods in our lives? How can we deal with our desire to serve other gods rather than the one true God?

- Read 1 John 1:9. Why is it important to keep our accounts with God short in order to maintain a right relationship?

- Read John 14:6. What must we do to come into a relationship with God? What must we believe about Jesus?

- Read Revelation 3:20. What does it mean for Christians to respond to Christ's knock, let Him in and eat with Him?

- Read John 1:12. What does it mean to become a child of God as it relates to our relationship with our own parents, or as parents ourselves with our own children?

ADDITIONAL DISCUSSION/ACTION STEPS

1. Ask if there is anyone who would like to receive Jesus Christ as his or her Savior. Ask if there are any group members who have made a recommitment to walk more consistently and/or more deeply with the Lord. Provide an opportunity to those who want to recommit to do so now.

3. End this time with group prayer for the new believers and for the new commitments.

TWO

PRAISE GOD AND REJOICE

Objective

To help group members understand that because of the hope and promises we have in Jesus, Christians can indeed "rejoice in the Lord always."

Preparation

EXERCISE

Obtain sheets of plain paper and pens or pencils, plus a whiteboard, chalkboard or flipchart and felt-tip pens or chalk.

DISCUSSION

Familiarize yourself with the questions in the following "Group Participation" section in the lesson, and choose which questions you definitely want to discuss with the group. If you haven't already done so for Exercise 1, obtain a whiteboard, chalkboard or flipchart and felt-tip pens or chalk.

Group Participation

EXERCISE

Divide the group in half and have them walk to opposite sides of the room. Give each group a sheet of paper and pen or pencil. Instruct the groups to read Psalm 106. Explain that Group A will list all the things the Lord did for the Israelites and Group B will list all the things the Israelites did instead of obeying God. After about five minutes, call the groups back together and have them share their findings. Write their lists on the board or chart as they share. Discuss why they think the Israelites kept turning away from God. Point out how He continued to love them, but that He also had to punish them for their wrongdoing. Also discuss how we continue to do similar things today.

DISCUSSION

1. Discuss the following questions (or the ones you have chosen) from the "A Closer Look at God's Truth" section:

    •   Read Philippians 1:1. What does it mean to be a bond servant/slave? To what are non-Christians enslaved?

    •   Read Philippians 1:3-8. Why was Paul thankful for the Philippian church? Read 2 Corinthians 8:1-8. What were their circumstances? What amazing thing did these churches do for other Christian churches?

    •   Read Romans 15:26-27. What were the Macedonian and Achaian churches' motivations for their sacrificial giving?

    •   Read Philippians 4:11-19. What were some of the things that had happened to Paul during the course of his ministry? What were his circumstances when he was writing this letter? What was his attitude according to verses 11-12?

    •   What is the warning that Paul gave in Philippians 2:14-18? How does complaining and arguing affect our witness to the world around us? How would being more joy-filled change the world's perception of Christians?

    •   What were Paul's words of encouragement in Philippians 3:1; 4:4? How can we "rejoice in the Lord always" while going through difficult circumstances?

2. Read Psalm 33:1-3; 50:23; 66:1,8; 81:1. What does each of these psalms teach us about having an attitude of gratitude?

ADDITIONAL DISCUSSION/ACTION STEPS

1. Invite group members to share their psalms of praise that they were asked to write at the conclusion of the session. Encourage them to share by reading your own psalm first.

2. Using the whiteboard, chalkboard or flipchart have the group write a psalm of praise together.

3. Share the small groups' personal psalms and conclude with a couple of praise songs.

THREE

OVERCOME WORRY

Objective

To help group members understand that worrying is a sign of a lack of trust in God and His promises and that we have the choice between trusting God or worrying about our situations.

Preparation

EXERCISE 1
Prepare a list of some of the silliest worries you have ever had or have heard from others.

EXERCISE 2
Obtain paper, pens or pencils and a watch or timer.

DISCUSSION
Familiarize yourself with the questions in the following "Group Participation" section and in the lesson, and choose which questions you definitely want to discuss with the group. Prepare for the last activity in the "A Closer Look at God's Truth" section by writing out Philippians 4:6-7 on a whiteboard, chalkboard or flipchart. (**Option:** Type the verse and run off copies for the group members.) Have paper and pens or pencils available to do the action step at the end of the session.

Group Participation

EXERCISE 1
Invite group members to share the silliest worry they have ever heard. Begin the sharing with one or two of your own that you have prepared ahead of time. Discuss how people can be overcome by worrying about things that they can do nothing about.

EXERCISE 2

Give each group member a piece of paper and a pen or pencil. Tell them that they will have a one-minute worry-a-thon. Instruct them that when you tell them "go," they are to write down everything that they have worried about in the past week no matter how minor the worry. Give them one minute to write their lists. At the end of one minute, tell them to stop writing. Instruct them to read over their list and put a star by any of their worst worries that came true. Also tell them to put a checkmark beside any situations they are still worrying about. Then instruct them to cross out any outcomes that didn't happen or that were more favorable than they thought. Instruct them to write the words of Philippians 4:6 across the whole list.

DISCUSSION

1. Discuss the following questions (or the ones you have chosen) from the "A Closer Look at God's Truth" section:

    *   Read Philippians 2:13. What are some ways that God works in believers to will and to work for His good pleasure?

    *   What were the circumstances in Paul's life as he wrote this letter to the Philippians? (*He was in prison, chained to a Roman guard; his future was uncertain; he could be executed at anytime.*)

    *   Read Philippians 1:19-20. How did Paul describe the difficulty of his situation? How did he affirm his trust in God in this passage? What was his ultimate goal?

    *   What are we *not* to trust in according to Philippians 3:3? What does it mean to trust in the flesh? (*Trusting in our own strengths and abilities to overcome difficulties.*) What dangers are there in putting confidence in the flesh? What are some examples of what happens when we trust in our own ability to overcome trials? Where should we put our trust, and why?

    *   Read Jeremiah 17:5-8. What does verse 5 say about the person who puts his trust in himself or in other people? What does trusting in ourselves say about our relationship with God? What will happen to the person who puts trust in his or her own abilities according to verse 6? How does that relate to his or her spiritual life? How is the person who

trusts in the Lord described? What is promised during times of trial? How does that relate to the spiritual life?

- Read Philippians 1:27-30. What are some ways that a person who is suffering for Christ might be blessed in the midst of that suffering? Invite volunteers to share how they have witnessed God's blessings in difficult times either in their own lives or in the lives of others.

- Have the entire group read Philippians 4:6-7 in unison. How is God's peace described in this passage? Invite volunteers to give examples of how they have experienced that supernatural peace. Read the passage in unison again. Encourage members to memorize the passage to remind them when they are tempted to give in to worry.

2. Read Isaiah 26:3-4. What are the conditions for being at peace? How can we keep our minds steadfast on the Lord? Why can we trust in the Lord to take care of our needs and worries?

ADDITIONAL DISCUSSION/ACTION STEPS

1. Spend some time helping group members memorize Philippians 4:6-7. If you have written the passage on the board or flipchart, you can use that now to have the group read it in unison several times and each time erase or black out a few words until the group can say it from memory.

2. Give the group members the opportunity to complete the activity suggested at the end of the "A Closer Look at My Own Heart" section.

3. Ask if anyone did the action step of writing out Isaiah 26:3-4 on an index card, writing the prayer on the reverse side of the card, and then reading it throughout the week. Invite volunteers to share what happened as they did this action during the week. Encourage those who haven't done the action step to do so.

4. Close with prayers of thanksgiving for God's faithfulness and provision. Invite members to pray aloud expressing their thanks and giving the Lord their worries.

ℛENEW YOUR MIND

Objective

To help group members understand that in order to renew our minds we must choose to daily put aside our old nature's thoughts and actions and work on nurturing the mind of Christ within us.

Preparation

EXERCISE

Collect several magazines and newspapers that contain articles or advertisements that demonstrate how the media preys on our minds, causing us to be dissatisfied with our present situations.

DISCUSSION

Familiarize yourself with the questions in the following "Group Participation" section and in the lesson, and choose which questions you definitely want to discuss with the group. Obtain several different Bible translations. Put a marker at Philippians 2:5 in each translation. Obtain a whiteboard, chalkboard or flipchart and felt-tip pens or chalk.

Cut 4" x 12" strips out of 12" x 18" sheets of construction paper—you will need approximately 10 strips. On each strip write a phrase from Philippians 4:8 until you have the whole verse written on the strips. Use these at the close of the session. You will also need to provide masking tape.

Invite one or two volunteers (you as the leader can be one of them) to be prepared to share how memorizing Scripture helps them renew their minds and train their thoughts to dwell on what is positive and Christ honoring, rather than negative and defeating.

Group Participation

EXERCISE I

Invite the group members to form groups of four or five. Provide each group with a couple of magazines or newspapers. Instruct them to browse through the magazines and newspapers to find articles or advertisements that demonstrate how the media and our culture entice us to become dissatisfied about our present situations or anxious about our futures. Give the groups about five minutes to find their best example and then have the whole group come together to share what they have found. As each small group shares their example, discuss how the world tempts us to be dissatisfied and anxious.

DISCUSSION

1. Discuss the following questions (or the ones you have chosen) from the "A Closer Look at God's Truth" section:

   - Read Philippians 1:12-18. What were the difficulties that Paul was experiencing? What were the positives that Paul discovered in these negative situations?

   - Read Ephesians 4:26-27. How does this passage relate to dwelling on good things? Is it wrong to get angry? How can we be angry yet not sin? How can anger give the devil a foothold?

   - Read Hebrews 12:14-15. If we continue to hold onto thoughts that make us angry, how does it affect our relationships? How can it affect a church? How does bitterness defile many?

   - Read Philippians 1:19-26. What positive aspects of death did Paul choose to dwell on? What were the positive aspects of continuing to live on earth that Paul focused on?

   - Read Philippians 2:5. What did Paul desire for the Philippians? How would believers' minds, doubts, forgiveness, fears, and general outlook be affected if they obeyed Philippians 2:5?

   - Read 2 Corinthians 10:3-5. What kind of battle is being described? What are the weapons that we can use? What is the power behind the weapons we can use?

   - Read Ephesians 6:10-18. What are some of the defenses/weapons that are described in this passage? Write each of these on the board or flipchart. How can these elements help us ward off the devil's implements of war? Why is the mind so important in a Christian's battle against Satan? How can we protect our minds with the truth?

- Read Romans 12:1-3 and Ephesians 4:17-24. On the left side of the board or chart write "The Unbeliever's Thoughts," and then draw a line from top to bottom and write "The Christian's Thoughts" on the other side of the line. What are the differences between the unbeliever's mind and the Christian's mind as described in the passages just read? (Write these observations on the chart.) How is the renewed mind related to the new self? How can we renew our minds daily? How can we help our new nature grow stronger than our old nature?

2. Discuss the following questions (or the ones you have chosen) from the "A Closer Look at My Own Heart" section:

   - Read John 5:5-9. How does this story about Jesus asking the paralytic if he wanted to be healed relate to us in our Christian growth?

   - Read Joshua 1:8 and Psalm 1:1-3. For those who regularly memorize Scripture, what benefits of the practice can they share with the group? What specific example can they give of how having Scripture memorized helped them change a negative situation into a positive one?

ADDITIONAL DISCUSSION/ACTION STEPS

1. To help group members memorize Philippians 4:8, distribute in random order to various group members the strips of paper that you have prepared ahead of time. Have the group members arrange them in the order they appear in the verse and tape them to the wall. Have the whole group read the verse two or three times. Then remove the phrases from the wall, but leave the tape attached. Mix up the order of the phrases. Divide the group into two smaller groups and have them compete to see which group can arrange the verse in the correct order the quickest.

2. Discuss ways in which we can use God's Word to help us deal with negative attitudes and thoughts. Encourage them to continue to memorize Scripture and to journal their thoughts regularly.

3. Close in prayer and reading (or saying from memory) Philippians 4:8.

$\mathscr{A}$PPROPRIATE CHRIST'S RIGHTEOUSNESS

Objective

To help group members understand that they cannot earn righteousness through their own efforts, but that they can only receive it through God's grace and their faith in Him to produce righteousness in their lives.

Preparation

EXERCISE

Make up a fictional calendar week for Nancy, who is described at the beginning of this week's study. Besides the activities mentioned in the example, add a few things that many women might encounter in a week (for instance, shopping, laundry, making meals, children's activities, and so forth). Type this calendar up and print a copy for each group member.

DISCUSSION

Familiarize yourself with the questions in the following "Group Participation" section and in the lesson, and choose which questions you definitely want to discuss with the group.

Group Participation

EXERCISE

Instruct the group members to read through Nancy's calendar listings. Discuss what she might do to bring more peace and contentment to her busy life. Ask if any group members have a similar calendar or have had one in the past and what they do to bring their busyness under control.

DISCUSSION

1. Discuss the following questions (or the ones you have chosen) from the "A Closer Look at God's Truth" section:

- Read Philippians 3:2-3, 2 Peter 2:1 and Jeremiah 9:25-26. How did Paul describe the false teachers and those who wanted to insist that Gentile Christians must be circumcised? What are the differences between those who are circumcised in the flesh only and those with circumcised hearts?

- Read Philippians 3:4-6. How did Paul describe his works in comparison to the works of others in verse 4? What were his previous acts of self-righteousness as given in verses 5-6?

- Read Philippians 3:7-9. How did Paul describe all his acts of self-righteousness? What must Christians count as lost—as rubbish—in order to gain Christ as Savior and Lord? Why is it impossible for humans to become righteous by doing good works? How will we know when we have done enough to gain true righteousness on our own?

- Read Philippians 3:10-11. What are the results of accepting Christ's righteousness? What did Paul mean by "knowing the power of [Christ's] resurrection"? Why do we need to consider our works as worthless in order to experience Christ's power?

- What does it mean to know "the fellowship of [Christ's] suffering"? In what ways are God's power perfected in our weaknesses? (Invite volunteers to share how they have experienced this in their own lives.) What part does realizing our own weaknesses play in accepting God's grace?

- Reread Philippians 3:10. What does it mean for a person to become like Jesus in His death? What is the result of being conformed to His death?

- Read Romans 6:1-14. What ways are we to be conformed to Christ's death? What are the results of putting the old self to death? In what ways does a Christian experience resurrection with Jesus? What is necessary for us to experience this resurrection?

- Read Philippians 1:2. What were the blessings of which Paul wrote? Who is the source of those blessings? Why is it necessary to accept God's grace before we can experience God's peace?

2. Discuss the following questions (or the ones you have chosen) from the "A Closer Look at My Own Heart" section:

   - Refer back to "Nancy's Calendar." If Nancy was a friend and she complained to you that she was not feeling very joyful about her many activities and even feeling resentful, how would you counsel her using what you have learned in this week's Bible study?

   - Read John 15:4-8. How does this word picture help you understand what is needed to produce eternal results in your life? How can we remain connected to the True Vine? How would being connected change your life? How would it change the lives of those around you—those in your sphere of influence?

Additional Discussion/Action Steps

1. Invite volunteers to share if they took one of the four options listed in the "Action Steps I Can Take Today" section. Ask them to share any results they have experienced from praying about the option they chose.

2. Continue to encourage group members to memorize Scripture and journal their thoughts and prayers.

3. Close the session by having the group members pray the prayer at the end of this week's study aloud together.

SIX

FORGET THE PAST

Objective

To help group members understand that they need to seek the forgiveness of those they have wronged, to forgive those who have wronged them and take care of any unresolved anger before they can continue on their path to spiritual maturity.

Preparation

EXERCISE
No preparation is needed.

DISCUSSION
Familiarize yourself with the questions in the following "Group Participation" section and in the lesson, and choose which questions you definitely want to discuss with the group. Obtain several different Bible translations. Put a marker at Philippians 3:12-14 in each translation.

Group Participation

EXERCISE
Divide the group into three smaller groups. Assign one of the scenarios from the "A Closer Look at the Problem" section to each of the groups. Have each group work together to suggest how they would counsel the woman about her situation. Have them answer the three questions for that woman. After a few minutes, bring the group back together and have each small group briefly summarize their suggestions.

DISCUSSION
1. Discuss the following questions (or the ones you have chosen) from the "A Closer Look at God's Truth" section:

- Read Philippians 3:7-14. What did Paul desire for his life? What was his ultimate goal? Why was it necessary for him to forget the past in order to reach his goal?

- Read 1 John 1:5-9. How can these verses remind us that we are forgiven and purified from all sin because of the blood Jesus shed for us?

- Read Matthew 5:23-24. Why are we commanded by God to forgive?

- Read Matthew 18:15-17. What are the steps in dealing with someone who has wronged us? Why did Jesus command us to first go privately to the person who has sinned against us?

- What does Matthew 18:21-22 teach about forgiving others? How is it possible to forgive someone who continues to wrong you?

2. Discuss the following questions (or the ones you have chosen) from the "A Closer Look at My Own Heart" section:

- Read 2 Corinthians 4:16. What does it mean for our "inner selves" to be renewed daily? What are some ways in which this can take place?

- What is the promise of Philippians 1:6? How long will this process take place? What are some ways in which we might restrict God's work to perfect us?

- Read Hebrews 10:24-25 and Galatians 6:2. How can we put these Scriptures into practice to help us mature in Christ?

ADDITIONAL DISCUSSION/ACTION STEPS

1. Have the group members pair up and spend time in prayer about any forgiveness they need to seek or unresolved anger issues that need to be dealt with. Encourage the prayer partners to contact each other during the week to keep them accountable to act on what needs to be done.

3. Close in prayer for the whole group. Make yourself available for anyone who might be struggling with issues brought up during the study.

SEVEN

OBEY GOD

Objective

To help group members understand that the only way to experience true joy and contentment is to live in obedience to God and that He will provide the strength we need to be obedient and keep us focused on our eternal home.

Preparation

EXERCISE 1

Prepare a list of commands for playing Simon Says. Put in a couple of really difficult commands, such as standing on one foot while doing another action, or keeping their arms in the air throughout the game. Prepare the list with the age and abilities of your group in mind. Practice giving the commands quickly.

EXERCISE 2

Obtain paper and pens or pencils. Also have a watch with a second hand or a timer.

DISCUSSION

Familiarize yourself with the questions in the following "Group Participation" section and in the lesson, and choose which questions you definitely want to discuss with the group.

Group Participation

EXERCISE 1

Play a game of Simon Says, giving the commands as quickly as possible. Make this fun. Continue to play until only one person is left in the game. Discuss the importance of obeying quickly, and some situations in which quick obedience is necessary for someone's health or safety. Relate this to obeying God and its effect on our joy and contentment. What are the advantages of obeying God immediately? What might happen if we do not obey Him immediately?

EXERCISE 2

Divide the group into smaller groups of four to six members each. Challenge the group to come up with a list of excuses that people use to explain away their bad behavior. Set the timer or note the time on the watch and give the groups about three minutes to make their lists. When time is up, call the whole group together and find out which group had the longest list. Have a representative from the winning group read their list. When the list is read, ask if there are any other excuses that the other small groups thought of that were not already mentioned. Discuss how even Christians will use these excuses to explain away their sin. Explain that we are all guilty of using excuses even if just to ourselves. Discuss how exasperating having a disobedient child can be to a parent and relate that to how God must feel about our own disobedience.

DISCUSSION

1. Discuss the following questions (or the ones you have chosen) from the "A Closer Look at God's Truth" section:

    • Read Acts 16:9-10 and 26:12-19. What do we learn about obeying God from Paul's actions? What do these two incidents tell us about Paul's relationship with the Lord?

    • Read Philippians 3:12-18. What does Paul mean in verse 16? (*Put into practice those truths you already understand.*) What two actions does he add in verse 17? What responsibilities do we have to those who may be watching us and following our example? How can Christians become enemies of the cross?

    • Read Philippians 2:12-16. Since we do not attain salvation by our good deeds, what does it mean "to work out [our] salvation with fear and trembling"? How did Paul commend the Philippians? What role does obedience play in working out our salvation? What is God's part in our growth and obedience? What should our attitude be as we obey God and what are the results of cheerful obedience?

- How does John 6:26-29 relate to working out our salvation?

- How does our disobedience affect others? What did Paul urge in Philippians 1:27-28? How would you describe a life that is lived in a manner that is worthy of the gospel? How does obedience help us stand firm in the Lord? How does obedience unite believers?

- What is the promise we find in 1 Corinthians 10:13 about God's power to help us overcome the temptations to sin? How does disobedience lead to our discontent and loss of joy?

- Read John 14:21. What is the demonstration of our love for Jesus? How does that relate to the relationship between a parent and a child?

- What does James 1:22-27 teach us about obedience?

- Read Philippians 3:18-21. How did Paul describe the motivation of the enemies of the cross? What should the Christian's motivation be and how does that relate to obedience?

2. Read Matthew 6:19-21. What are our treasures in heaven? In what ways can we store up heavenly or eternal treasures?

ADDITIONAL DISCUSSION/ACTION STEPS

1. Read Colossians 3:1-2. In what ways do our material, earthly possessions possess us, rather than the other way around?

2. What do Romans 8:18; 2 Corinthians 4:16–5:10; Philippians 1:21-23; 3:10-11,14 say about what our goals should be? How will our focus on these goals help us obey God? How will those goals affect our level of joy and contentment?

3. Encourage group members to set a spiritual goal for the next twelve months. If they haven't done so already, invite them to find an accountability partner among the group members.

4. Spend time memorizing Philippians 4:13 (or another appropriate verse from the study). Encourage members to appropriate this verse during the week when they are tempted to disobey the Lord's leading. Close in prayer.

EIGHT

Set Proper Priorities and Develop Your Ministry

Objective

To help group members understand that they must give the Lord first priority in their lives in order to experience true contentment. Also, help group members discover their spiritual gifts and learn how to use those gifts to bring others to the Lord.

Preparation

Exercise

During the week, call group members and ask them to bring their appointment calendars or to write out a schedule of their activities for this week. Write the Exercise questions on the board, a posterboard or flipchart page.

Discussion

Familiarize yourself with the questions in the following "Group Participation" section and in the lesson, and choose which questions you definitely want to discuss with the group. Obtain a whiteboard, chalkboard or flipchart and felt-tip pens or chalk. Note that there is a lot of material to cover in this session, so one suggestion might be to divide the whole group into smaller groups and assign one or two bullet points for each small group.

Group Participation

Exercise

Divide whole group into smaller groups of three or four members. Instruct the small groups to look at their calendars or schedules and answer the following questions:

- What does your calendar/schedule indicate to you about where your priorities are focused?
- Which events/duties distract you from following God?
- Do you schedule time to spend with God on your calendar?
- Where do you sense that you need to change activities to better serve the Lord?

Invite the group back together and discuss what they have learned from this activity about setting God-honoring priorities.

DISCUSSION

1. As time allows, discuss the following questions (or the ones you have chosen) from Part One of this study:

    - Read 2 Corinthians 5:9. How did Paul's goal in life affect his relationships, priorities and level of contentment?

    - Read Philippians 2:1-11. What are the similarities between Paul's life goal and Jesus' life goal?

    - How does Philippians 2:4 relate to what Jesus became when He dwelt on earth? Who did He do this for and why? How would you define "humility"?

    - Read John 15:9-13. What did Jesus promise His followers? What was the condition for the fulfillment of this promise? What is the commandment given in verse 12, and how does it relate to verses 10 and 11?

    - Read John 17:21-23. What is the main focus of this prayer? (*Unity of the church.*) What part does giving and accepting Christlike love play in perfecting us as Christians?

    - Read Hebrews 10:24-25. What motivates most people to go to church? (*Many go for the social aspects or to have their needs met.*) What is God's purpose for us as we meet together according to this Scripture passage? What are some ways that other believers have stimulated our love toward others?

2. As time allows, discuss the following questions (or the ones you have chosen) from Part Two of this study:

- Read Philippians 1:21-26. What does this passage reveal about Paul's love and unselfishness? How did Paul describe Timothy in Philippians 2:19-24? What were Timothy's motives for service?

- Read 2 Corinthians 9:6-15. What should be our attitude toward giving? What are some of the things that God may want us to give cheerfully? What are the blessings and rewards of giving generously and cheerfully?

- Read Matthew 5:9 and 2 Corinthians 5:18-21. What is promised to peacemakers? How could peacemaking function as a witness to nonbelievers? How can our ministry of peacemaking reconcile others to God? What is the function of ambassadors in world government? How does that relate to Christians being Christ's ambassadors?

- Read Ephesians 6:18-20. Who did Paul encourage the Ephesians to pray for? What did he specifically ask them to pray for regarding his own ministry?

- Read 2 Timothy 3:14-17. What have you learned from this study that you will use to more effectively minister to others?

ADDITIONAL DISCUSSION/ACTION STEPS

1. Read 1 Corinthians 13:4-7 and 1 John 3:17-18. Point out the obvious—that it isn't easy to always love others as described in this passage. Discuss how we can love others as Christ loves us.

2. Reread Philippians 1:20-21. Ask group members to prayerfully consider how their priorities compare to those of Paul. Discuss how their tomorrows will be different because of the priorities that they are choosing today.

3. Invite group members to share one Scripture passage from this study of Philippians that has especially spoken to them. Ask them to share what changes their chosen verse has brought into their lives.

4. Conclude this session with a time of worship and thanksgiving. Invite members to share prayers of thanksgiving. End by praying for the whole group using Philippians 1:9-11.

HAT IS AGLOW INTERNATIONAL?

From one nation to 172 worldwide...
From one fellowship to more than 4,600...
From 100 people to more than 17 million...

Aglow International has experienced phenomenal growth since its inception more than 40 years ago. In 1967, four women from the state of Washington prayed for a way to reach out to other Christian women in simple fellowship, free from denominational boundaries.

The first meeting held in Seattle, Washington, USA, drew more than 100 women to a local hotel. From that modest beginning, Aglow International has become one of the largest intercultural, interdenominational Christian organizations in the world.

Each year, an estimated 17 million people are ministered to through Aglow's local fellowship meetings, Bible studies, support groups, retreats, conferences and various outreaches. From the inner city to the upper echelons, from the next door neighbor to the corporate executive, Aglow seeks to minister to the felt needs of women and men around the world.

Christian women and men find Aglow a "safe place" to grow spiritually and begin to discover and use the gifts, talents and abilities God has given them. Aglow offers excellent leadership training and varied opportunities to develop those leadership skills.

Undergirding the evangelistic thrust of the ministry is an emphasis on prayer, which has led to an active prayer network linking six continents. The vast prayer power available through Aglow women and men around the world is being used by God to influence countless lives in families, communities, cities and nations.

$\mathcal{A}$GLOW'S MISSION STATEMENT IS . . .

- To help restore and mobilize women and men around the world

- To promote gender reconciliation in the Body of Christ as God designed

- To amplify awareness of global concerns from a biblical perspective

---

$\mathcal{A}$GLOW'S THREE MANDATES

1. To promote gender reconciliation between male and female in the Body of Christ as God designed.

2. To answer God's call to minister to the Muslim people, while bringing awareness of the basic theological differences between Islam and Christianity.

3. To stand in loving support for Israel and the Jewish people, while helping to bring awareness to the Body of Christ concerning God's plans and purposes for those people He calls the "apple of His eye."

ℋGLOW MINISTERS IN . . .

Albania, Angola, Anguilla, Antigua, Argentina, Aruba, Australia, Austria, Bahamas, Bahrain, Barbados, Belarus, Belgium, Belize, Benin, Bermuda, Bolivia, Botswana, Brazil, Britain, Bulgaria, Burkina Faso, Cameroon, Canada, Chile, China, Colombia, Congo (Dem. Rep. of), Congo (Rep. of), Costa Rica, Côte d'Ivoire, Cuba, Curaçao, Czech Republic, Denmark, Djibouti, Dominica, Dominican Republic, Ecuador, Egypt, El Salvador, Equatorial Guinea, Estonia, Ethiopia, Faroe Islands, Fiji, Finland, France, Gabon, the Gambia, Germany, Ghana, Grand Cayman, Greece, Grenada, Guam, Guatemala, Guinea, Guyana, Haiti, Honduras, Hungary, Iceland, India, Indonesia, Ireland, Israel, Jamaica, Japan, Kenya, Korea, Kyrgyzstan, Latvia, Lithuania, Malawi, Malaysia, Mali, Mauritius, Mexico, Mongolia, Mozambique, Myanmar, Nepal, Netherlands, New Zealand, Nicaragua, Niger, Nigeria, Norway, Oman, Pakistan, Panama, Papua New Guinea, Peru, Philippines, Portugal, Puerto Rico, Romania, Russia, Rwanda, Samoa, Samoa (American), Scotland, Senegal, Serbia, Sierra Leone, Singapore, South Africa, Spain, Sri Lanka, St. Kitts, St. Lucia, St. Maartan, St. Vincent, Sudan, Suriname, Sweden, Switzerland, Tajikistan, Tanzania, Thailand, Togo, Tonga, Trinidad/ Tobago, Turks & Caicos Islands, Uganda, Ukraine, United States, Uruguay, Uzbekistan, Venezuela, Vietnam, Virgin Islands (American), Virgin Islands (British), Wales, Yugoslavia, Zambia, Zimbabwe, and other nations.

To find your nearest Aglow Fellowship, call or write us at:

P.O. Box 1749, Edmonds, WA 98020-1749
Phone: 425-775-7282 or 1-800-793-8126
Fax: 425-778-9615 / Email: aglow@aglow.org
Website: http://www.aglow.org/